Eurhythmics for Young Children

Six Lessons for Winter

Monica Dale

Musi**K**inesis

Published by MusiKinesis
Ellicott City, Maryland

Copyright © Monica Dale 2000

ISBN 0-9701416-1-0

Library of Congress Card Number: 00-191220

Monica Dale
3734 Cross Bow Court
Ellicott City, MD 21042

Contents

I ask myself: "Am I content, I whose task it is to educate tiny children and prepare them for the future?" Confronted with this question, we are all sometimes constrained to bow the head in silence. On the other hand, when we are able to leave the class with the feeling that we have given of our best, and have done all we could to put before the coming generation an ideal towards which we, for the most part, have but vainly tried to reach, then we can exclaim with conviction and in all earnestness: "Yes, I am content, perfectly content." † 105

Emile Jaques-Dalcroze

Introduction

For many years in music education methods classes in higher education the pedagogical approaches of Carl Orff, Zoltan Kodaly and Emile Jaques-Dalcroze have been cited as important methodologies for introducing children to basic concepts of musicianship. While the Orff and Kodaly approaches have been widely adopted in elementary classrooms throughout the United States, the Dalcroze approach has been used infrequently due to the relatively few opportunities for college students in teacher training programs to learn about the method.

With the publication of *Eurhythmics for Young Children* by Monica Dale, there is now structured material that allows music teachers working with young children the opportunity to incorporate Dalcroze methodology in their teaching. Incorporating Eurhythmics, solfege, and piano improvisation, the three branches of Dalcroze study, Ms. Dale integrates these approaches into complete lessons focusing on important fundamental music concepts. Realizing that not all music teachers will have developed the improvisational piano skills needed for teaching in the Dalcroze approach, the author has presented initial accompaniments in the body of the text and full-fledged song accompaniments in the appendix. Most importantly, each lesson proceeds in a highly structured fashion always maintaining focus on the important principle of presenting the music first and then proceeding to the theoretical concept.

Six Lessons for Winter is a logical second volume to the initial publication, *Six Lessons for Fall.* This second volume adds the concepts of anapest, compound meter, and meters of three and four to the basic musical concepts found in the first volume. The appendix also contains supplementary worksheets which allow the teacher to begin to transfer aural concepts of pitch to staff notation using highly original visual models.

Eurhythmics for Young Children needs to find its way into the hands of music teachers for young children to allow these students to experience the joy of musical discovery, which the philosophy and method originated by Emile Jaques-Dalcroze allows to happen in a very natural way.

Arthur E. Ostrander, Dean
Ithaca College
School of Music

Acknowledgements

Many thanks to the people who made this book possible:

Arthur E. Ostrander, Dean of the School of Music, Ithaca College.

John R. Stevenson, a musician and pedagogue of great genius who I was blessed to have as my teacher and mentor.

Michael Pantano, husband and support system extraordinaire.

Hilary Dale Johnson, my daughter, who taught me child development firsthand.

Claire and William Dale, duo-pianists who fostered my love of music through nature, nurture, and parental patience.

My students past and present, who continue to teach me how to teach.

All Eurhythmics teachers who've paved the way by developing the method and creating ideas that have been passed down over the years.

Overview

About Eurhythmics

Three Branches

Emile Jaques-Dalcroze (1865-1950) developed a unique approach to music education comprised of three interrelated branches:

Eurhythmics: Study of music involving kinesthetic exercises, particularly addressing rhythm, meter, phrase, form, dynamics, and agogic nuance.

Solfege: Study of pitch, melody, and harmony through singing, eartraining, and theory, incorporating music concepts and teaching strategies of Eurhythmics.

Piano improvisation: The spontaneous synthesis of Eurhythmics and Solfege experience at the instrument.

The three branches are not discrete, but are inherently connected through their philosophical basis. They overlap in both content and practice, and each involves all parameters of music.

Three Principles

Pedagogical processes within each branch involve the same core tenets of the method, most notably:

Theory Follows Practice: Music concepts are made concrete through direct, active experience of ear, mind and body. It is through this experience that abstract notational symbols and analysis hold musical meaning.

Listening: Music as sound permeates music education through the Dalcroze method. Even notation, as a representation of sound, comes to provides aural – not merely visual – meaning.

Improvisation: Students improvise to deepen and demonstrate their music experience and understanding, in the same way that speaking concretizes a working knowledge of vocabulary, syntax and content. In addition, the teacher improvises during the lesson both musically and pedagogically, making the process flexible and responsive to the students.

A Contemporary Perspective

Through his own teaching, Jaques-Dalcroze structured a new framework for music pedagogy. He left behind essays on his developing thoughts and forward-looking philosophy, and infinite potential for further development. Today his writings, particularly those collected in *Rhythm, Music and Education,* are the definitive reference for Eurhythmicians. A century after they were written, his words are interpreted through practice in various ways. Thus in a sense, Jaques-Dalcroze's legacy is more a philosophy than a "method" in the strict sense of the word. That his work lives beyond his own time and culture demonstrates its marvelous adaptability.

Because his work was passed on from mentor to student, the greatest gift Jaques-Dalcroze left us was an ancestry of proteges. As they in turn taught new generations, Jaques-Dalcroze's inspiration spread through the 20th century, branching out to influence modern dance, theatre, scenic design, gymnastics, creative movement, and above all, music education. Through a century of change and development in arts and arts education, Eurhythmics teachers have contributed personal innovations to the method and passed them on to their students. Today, a breadth of practical approaches to the method has naturally developed, while Eurhythmicians continue to share a common philosophical basis.

The interpretation of Jaques-Dalcroze's work that I embrace was taught to me by John R. Stevenson. In my analysis, it is both traditional and innovative – adhering to Jaques-Dalcroze's educational principles, while taking the wings he gave us to explore and expand those principles in creative practice toward contemporary needs and goals.

A humanist, child-centered, logically-layered progression of concepts and skill development maintains Jaques-Dalcroze's roots in the pedagogical philosophies of Rousseau and Pestalozzi, and even further back to the ancient Greeks. Interestingly, these ideas comply with educational theorists including Piaget, Dewey and Bruner, and continue to match with "new" notions such as "cooperative learning," "critical thinking" and "multiple learning modes."

This approach organizes the curriculum by specific music subjects, developed through the skills that create and signify thorough understanding. It demands physical technique and sound musicianship of its teachers, allows for creative joy and personal innovations, and adheres steadfastly to its primary objective: music education.

About This Book

The *Eurhythmics for Young Children* series is intended not only as a practical resource for Eurhythmics teachers, but also as examples of one approach to the Dalcroze method for pedagogical study and analysis. It is designed to provide lessons of logically-sequenced activities in order to illustrate the development of skills and content, both within each lesson and across a series of lessons.

Teaching through the Dalcroze approach is much like cooking without recipes. For success, we must learn how to create improvisationally. Experience in the method teaches us various combinations, patterns, strategies, and techniques, which we then become free to recombine in our own unique way. And as any improvisational cook knows, no two results are quite the same.

The *Eurhythmics for Young Children* books are, in that sense, pedagogical cookbooks. They present examples of ways of working which teachers might add to their repertoire, with the freedom to vary and develop the ideas through their own creativity.

These lessons represent one approach to a complex and diverse method. Because Eurhythmics varies according to each teacher's individual experiences, skills, and preferences, this book simply reflects one teacher's personal perspectives and practices, and does not presume to be a definitive work.

"Six Lessons for Winter" continues the lessons from "Six Lessons for Fall." However, as concepts are reviewed before being developed, a teacher could well begin with the lessons in this book.

Jaques-Dalcroze Sources

The quotes from Jaques-Dalcroze are taken from two collections of his articles, cited by symbol and page number:

* Jaques-Dalcroze, Emile. *Rhythm, Music and Education.* Translated by Harold F. Rubenstein. Reprint Ed., London: The Dalcroze Society, 1980.

† Jaques-Dalcroze, Emile. *Eurhythmics, Art and Education.* Edited by Cynthia Cox, translated by Frederick Rothwell. Reprint Ed., Salem, New Hampshire: Ayer Co., 1985.

x

Structure of the Book

Each lesson is formatted as follows:

Lesson: Music Subject

Activity

Procedure   Notes

Music Subject: This approach to Eurhythmics organizes lessons by music content. Because the lessons generally build upon previous skills and concepts, the subject titles given refer to the new or primary music subjects of the lesson. Other topics, including music concepts from previous lessons, specific physical skills, and extra-musical themes, are included in each lesson on a secondary level of emphasis.

As no lesson completely exhausts its subject matter, further lessons on each subject might well ensue before the next one. Concepts should be continually revisited and developed in a spiral fashion. This allows time for children's own development, carries known skills over to new ones, brings new understanding to enlighten familiar ideas, and allows musical variety in the process. For example, while "Six Lessons for Fall" includes an introductory lesson in compound meter, the subject is revisited in more depth in this book.

Activity: This column outlines the progression of each lesson.

Procedure: Each activity is described in detail.

Notes: These sidebars provide information such as rationale, alternative approaches, ideas for development, and further details.

Introductory Outline: Each lesson is preceded by an outline showing the sequence of activities and their primary purposes, and listing materials needed.

Supplementary Worksheets: These are provided as options to reinforce each lesson, provide a springboard for children to discuss their experiences with their parents, and to develop notational skills. They are discussed further in the next section.

Additional Accompaniments: The Appendix provides arrangements of songs that appear in the lesson units without accompaniments.

Elements in the Lessons

Movement

In the Eurhythmics class, movement is not taught for its own sake, but rather as a vehicle for experiencing music. When I teach dance, I am concerned with shape, line, technique, and specific movement vocabulary; but because teaching Eurhythmics means teaching music, physical skills are refined solely in order to enhance musical experience. Because the instrument of Eurhythmics is the whole person – body, mind and spirit – part of our task is to "tune" and integrate the instrument for optimal learning. This creates benefits of value to musicianship and beyond it as well, such as enhanced concentration, memory, coordination, and spatial awareness.

These Eurhythmics lessons incorporate movement techniques designed to embody specific music concepts, and opportunities for improvised movement in relation to music.

Rhythmic Notation

When movement embodies specific rhythms, notation is easily introduced as a visual representation of physical, rhythmic experience. While the experiences in "Six Lessons for Fall" remained primarily experiential, "Six Lessons for Winter" introduces fundamental notation to represent experience, reinforced through games and exercises. This is particularly valuable for children at the ages when they are able or beginning to read.

Rhythmic Modes

Jaques-Dalcroze adopted the rhythmic modes, originated by the ancient Greeks, for his method. This book includes the trochaic (long-short) and anapest (short-short-long) modes. These lessons don't yet identify the rhythms to the children using the Greek names, but rather with words that relate directly to their movement experiences.

When truly functioning as modes, the rhythmic patterns are underlying impulses within music composition. A piece may be composed in a rhythmic mode in the same way it is composed in a tonal mode (dance forms provide the most obvious examples). Here, however, they are treated as patterns – means of grouping durations so that an entire rhythm is perceived, rather than sensing only one duration at a time. This approach allows for a more musical performance than mechanically reading from note to note. As patterns, the modes help develop rhythmic perception, identification, reading, and notation, all related to musical experience in movement.

As with all concepts taught, the teacher should have a thorough experience and understanding of the modes to convey them to students.

Melodic Studies

In his 1925 article "The Inner Technique of Rhythm," Jaques-Dalcroze wrote:

> *There are two physical agencies through which we appreciate and understand, live and experience music: the ear, as regards sound; the entire nervous system, as regards rhythm. Experience proves that it is not easy to educate both of these simultaneously. A child finds it difficult to apprehend a melodic succession and the rhythm animating it at the same time. Before teaching the relations between sound and movement, it is wise to study these two elements separately. Sound is manifestly of secondary importance since it has not its origin and model within ourselves; whereas movement is instinctive in man, and therefore first in importance. And so I begin musical studies by the methodical and experimental teaching of movement.* [†51]

This rationale explains the emphasis on rhythmic movement experience through Eurhythmics first, and the inclusion of pitch studies secondly. My lessons, therefore, focus on rhythm and pitch separately, but simultaneously. I see them as two parallel lines of study that cross and overlap, interrelating on their way toward complete integration.

For example, children's singing is always based on the metric and/or rhythmic subjects of the Eurhythmics lesson. Songs introduced at the beginning of lessons serve as springboards from which rhythmic elements are discovered and then studied further; singing activities at the end of lessons are designed to integrate and apply skills and concepts of Eurhythmics to pitch.

However, activities in perceiving, identifying, or notating musical elements treat rhythm and pitch separately at first, with specific attention to only one area at a time.

Pitch Notation

The notation of pitch carries its own unique challenges for young children. As the Dalcroze approach moves teachers to respond to our students and develop approaches creatively, the means of addressing pitch notation in this book are the result of my own observations.

In my experience, children need to gain skills in notating and identifying line and space note positions as a third parallel study. Initially, I approach elements of pitch notation as a representation of *movement* experiences within lines and spaces, and then later link notation skills to melodic studies.

The first objectives, in my approach, are to teach children to differentiate line and space notes, to identify notes' positions on a staff, and to develop basic note-drawing skills. These abilities are prerequisite to notating their experiences of seconds, represented in a line-space pattern.

The next steps, developed in "Six Lessons for Spring," are to begin distinguishing seconds and repeated pitches aurally, notate them, and identify them using numbers, note names, and solfege syllables. These are early, fundamental skills in melodic dictation and sight-singing.

Supplementary Worksheets

"Six Lessons for Winter" introduces written sheets to provide reinforcement of lessons and development of writing skills, within the class, at home, or both. They also create opportunities for children to relate their lesson experiences to their parents. The very act of recalling and explaining activities reinforces the experiences.

The worksheets are ideal for children at the ages when they are learning to read. As this may not occur until Kindergarten and above, they are certainly optional for preschoolers.

Stories

Stories aren't a necessary part of Eurhythmics lessons, but I include them for several reasons. First, by requiring improvisation and/or direct response to music, they can help to develop and reinforce skills. Second, they provide a way to culminate a sequence of learning. Finally, children love stories, and whenever we can captivate their imaginations, we've truly connected with them.

Songs

In the context of specific lessons, the piano may or may not be required to accompany songs. However, the songs are given in the Appendix with accompaniment to provide the option of using the piano with them. The accompaniments given are suggestions, and the teacher may certainly create new ones.

Improvisation

The Eurhythmics teacher's responsiveness to the students allows them to have creative input in the lesson, making the process itself inherently improvisatory. In addition, Eurhythmics lessons naturally include improvisatory activity in singing and movement. At this level, such forms of improvisation may well suffice; however, for teachers who want to include more work with instruments, the experiences in these lessons are excellent preparation for instrumental improvisation.

Piano Improvisation Examples

The sample ideas for the piano are presented as starting points and illustrations. The teacher should feel free to create original ideas or to use these examples for further expansion and development.

Jaques-Dalcroze Quotes

See page ix for source citations.

The Teacher's Experience

No book can take the place of direct, personal experience in the Dalcroze method. Just as students learn through experience, teachers must also gain first-hand experience in the method to develop the skills, understanding, and deep intuition needed to teach Eurhythmics. While all teachers can get ideas from this book, to make practical use of it, Eurhythmics training is essential.

Musical skills are the key elements to Dalcroze teacher training. In order to teach them, we must have them in our very bones. For each exercise a teacher leads students to perform, the teacher needs command of a multiplicity of skills gained through Dalcroze studies. These include not only a clear working knowledge of all parameters of music, but also the extra-musical skills that Dalcroze studies develop: coordination, quick reactions, concentration, memory, and physical technique.

Pedagogical skills are the most advanced outgrowth of Dalcroze training. By learning through the method, studying its philosophical principles, analyzing its applications, and practice-teaching under a mentor, teachers learn to think in a Dalcrozian way. This is the underpinning that gives each moment of a lesson its clear pedagogical purpose. Moreover, it is the only way to achieve the spontaneity important to teaching creatively through Eurhythmics, as discussed further below.

Piano improvisation, combining musical and pedagogical skills, is an important tool to develop for Eurhythmics. While this book presupposes skill in this area, sample ideas for the piano are presented as starting points and illustrations. What's important is not just what the teacher plays, but how. Experience in the method enables the teacher to sense music and movement simultaneously, and to move vicariously with the class in creating music with the articulation, tempo, and phrasing that embodies each exercise.

Personal Notes on Structure and Procedure

While Eurhythmics teachers share a philosophical basis, we each have our own ways of teaching. Like the rest of this book, the following notes are part "method" and part personal preference based on my experience.

Bare feet

Bare feet are important to freedom of movement in the Eurhythmics class. Where possible, establish a routine for the children of leaving their shoes and socks lined up along one wall. In conservatory situations where parents can supervise their removal and replacement, leaving shoes outside the classroom saves time for lessons and allows quick transitions between classes.

Classroom

Ideally, floors for Eurhythmics are like dance studio floors – sprung, preferably wood, with street shoes forbidden – but few of us have such pristine conditions. I sweep floors myself if necessary rather than forgo bare feet. Hard linoleum over concrete requires careful attention to technique in landing from jumps and leaps to prevent physical strain or injury.

Carpeting inhibits many movements, such as sliding, and can even cause rug-burns. However, in rooms where there is a small rug that can't be rolled up, I've used it to provide a focal point for gathering children together at points during a lesson, and to delineate an area to move around in a circle.

Keep the piano close to the area where the children begin the lesson and are likely to carry out most activity. If the room is very large, I wouldn't have the piano at a far end where the children can get too distant. I'd rather that they move around me. Staying close to the piano also facilitates your own transitions between playing and moving, saving the time it takes to run that 20-yard dash.

Other than materials needed for the lesson, in my opinion, the room is best kept empty. Visual vacancy allows greater focus on aural stimuli and movement. While it's a common expectation in some schools for every inch of every wall to be decorated with bright posters and such, I find them a sensory distraction to the children and myself.

Ritual

Removing shoes and socks is one part of a class ritual. My classes for young children always begin seated in a circle with a physical "warm-up" related to the lesson, and conclude in the circle with the same ending song. The sense of ritual provided by this repetition prepares mind and body for the Eurhythmics class as a special experience, helping students to transition into the unique environment of the Eurhythmics class, and to close each experience with a comforting cadence.

Quick-Reaction Exercises:

While several Eurhythmics teaching techniques reoccur in varying contexts, the "Quick Reaction" exercise is one that merits special explanation. The purpose of this strategy is to enhance the efficiency of the ear-mind-body connection, developing the control that allows for true spontaneity in music-making. Moreover, quick reaction exercises are an effective way to contrast ideas and clarify relationships (such as ratios of beat, division, and multiple, for example).

Quick-reaction exercises are *not* meant to trick students. These exercises should be led sensitively to provide just the right level of challenge, allowing the students opportunities to succeed, and gradually increasing in difficulty. To trip students up creates a nervous, jarring and disorganized feeling in ear, mind and body, and does not lead to the control for which the exercises are designed.

Every quick-reaction exercise must take into account the physical preparation needed for a movement change, and allow sufficient time for the "command." For example, imagine being directed to leap on an accented beat. You might be able to leap *after* the accented beat for a sort of canonic effect, but not *on* it. Why? Because a leap requires an important physical preparation (bending the knees and brushing a leg forward), as well as suspension and landing. Trying to leap with the accent would require a late, rushed preparation, producing a sense of being *out* of physical control and *off* of the music – precisely the opposite of our intent.

Discipline

The optimal experience of Eurhythmics requires freedom — freedom of thought, freedom of movement, freedom of self. Too many adults have well-developed inner censors, criticizing and obstructing their physical and musical instincts, and holding back the part of themselves that is most free to experience and express music — their wild "inner child," if you will. For them, a teaching environment needs to convey safety and trust of both the environment and themselves.

Children, however, are naturally free – their wild instincts effervesce and bump up against boundaries. Certainly they do need boundaries, and on some level they know that it's more fun to play when there are a few rules. I believe that the trick to teaching children is to provide boundaries that give enough reach for them to be themselves. Soon enough, the world will "civilize" them, at best without developing those inner censors that tell them not to trust their instincts.

There is a balance of order and chaos — the order of a group learning experience, and the chaos of creativity and natural joy. As any teacher knows, you cannot accept the five-year-old boys' penchant for pouncing upon each other and turn it into a learning experience — some instincts just won't work in class and need to stay on the playground. However, there is no need to control young children with constant reprimands, maintain their total silence, or fit the children to our own order rather than the other way around. The balance between order and chaos will vary among teachers, but in teaching Eurhythmics, should always allow children to be children.

Spontaneity

Have I ever taught a lesson *exactly* like one in this book? Probably not! After all, children were present, and that makes anything unpredictable. Moreover, there is the matter of the clock. While these lessons are designed for approximately 45 minutes, it does no good to rush in an effort to fit everything in, or to repeat exercises *ad nauseum* to fill time. It's important to be able to adapt as needed, flexibly following the unique development of each class.

Planning is good, but digression can be even better. In fact, many of the ideas in this book stemmed from specific interactions with children. Anyone who intends to make practical use of the ideas in this book should strive to develop ideas further, create original classwork, and respond improvisationally to their own students.

The musical skills, creative ability, and improvisational spontaneity to respond to children in teaching are all developed through Dalcroze training. This combination of tools and open responsiveness makes children complete participants in the lesson, and ensures that the curriculum is tailored to the child and not the other way around. Moreover, it makes every teaching experience a new learning experience for the teacher.

Eurhythmics teaching can develop, refine and inspire all of your own musical and creative skills, especially when you let your students teach you. Young children are the best teachers, because they tell you exactly what you're doing wrong. For example, after training by teaching Eurhythmics to properly-quiet college students, my first job as a Eurhythmician was teaching kindergarten and first grade music throughout a public school district in New York. As I listened to and watched the children, they taught me everything from the obvious matters my blatant inexperience missed ("This music is too fast to skip to!" "I can't sing that low!") to structure ("Hey, we haven't sung a song in awhile") to pacing (finishing an exercise by collapsing on the floor = "We're tired, it's time to settle down a bit"; interacting with each other and not the activity = "We're done with this, why aren't you?").

Following children's lead can teach us many things – how to organize and pace the rhythm of a lesson, how to adjust tempi for their movement and pitch for their voices, how to arrive at the right level of challenge, how to articulate music at the piano to elicit specific movement qualities. But above all, it teaches us a means to learn more, because being responsive is a skill that grows with practice. The more skilled we become in being responsive, the more we continue to learn from our students every step of the way, with deepening insight, in our own never-ending spiral of growth.

The main thing to remember is that the function of parents and teachers is to strengthen and develop the child in such fashion that mind and body form a perfect instrument whereon to learn to play the song of life. [†101]

Emile Jaques-Dalcroze

Lesson One

Beat, Division and Multiple

Experiences of beat, division and multiple, whether introductory or as a review
from "Six Lessons for Fall," Lesson Two; beginning notation of beat, division and multiple;
introducing a first element of pitch notation: identification of spaces between lines.

Materials

1. Tiny bears (optional)

2. Three prepared cards with beat, division, and multiple

3. Five lengths of ribbon, yarn or other material

4. Supplementary Worksheets, #1 (optional)

2

Lesson One: Beat, Division and Multiple

Outline

I. Warm-up with beat, division, multiple ....Preparation; introduction of concepts

II. Song: "Listen, Little Brown Bears" ....Engages children; incorporates concepts

III. Moving the multiple (as bears)
    A. With drum and teacher ....Focus on physical experience of duration
    B. With the piano music ....Association with music in sound
    C. Stopping/starting with verbal cues ....Quick reaction (excitation/inhibition)
    D. Following the piano to stop/start ....Aural perception; quick reaction

IV. Moving the division (as squirrels)
    A. With drum and teacher ....Focus on physical experience of divisions
    B. With the piano ....Association with music in sound
    C. Stopping/starting ....Quick reaction (excitation/inhibition)
    D. Arm movements ("digging") ....Adding differentiation of body parts
    E. Alternations following piano ....Aural perception of registers; quick reaction

V. Alternating multiple and division
    A. With verbal cues from piano ....Quick reaction; association with music
    B. Responding to piano only ....Aural perception of music for response

VI. Story: "The Bears and the Squirrels"
    A. Responding with individual roles ....Isolating division and multiple
    B. Enacting the story with words ....Association with music
    C. Enacting with music only ....Aural perception; responding to music

VII. Adding the beat (as deer)
    A. With drum and teacher ....Focus on physical experience of beat
    B. With the piano ....Association with music in sound

VIII. Alternations of beat, division, multiple
    A. All three roles ....Aural perception; Quick reactions
    B. Taking individual roles ....Differentiation of beat, division, multiple
    C. Identifying others' roles ....Movement perception; awareness of others; memory
    D. Responding to arm positions ....Visual perception for quick reactions

IX. Transferring to sound
    A. "Stepping" hands on floor" ....Linking kinesthetic experience to sound
    B. Clapping ....Transferring "steps" on floor to sound

X. Notation
    A. With spatial levels ....Transferring exercise with arm positions
    B. Without spatial levels ....Reading notation alone

XI. Stepping the Scale forward and back ....Kinesthetic experience of scale directions

XII. Pitch Pre-notation: lines on floor
    A. Stepping across spaces ....Kinesthetic experience of line/space differentiation; Association with sound
    B. Jumping to/identifying numbers ....Awareness/differentiation of spaces by number
    C. Jumping to numbers called ....Pre-notation of spaces by position/number

XIII. Supplementary Worksheets (optional) ....Reinforcement of lesson

XIV. Ending Song ....Closure

Lesson One: Beat, Division and Multiple

Warm-Up

Begin with children sitting in a circle, legs straight and feet pointing in toward the center.

Provide warm-up exercises to a steady beat, twice as fast, and twice as slow.

For example:

The warm-up introduces concepts to be explored in the lesson.

Movements might include pointing and flexing feet, hugging knees and releasing legs forward again, curving and straightening spine, dropping head side to side, lifting shoulders up and down, etc.

Point, flex, point flex,   point,   flex,   etc...

Song: "Listen, Little Brown Bear"

Briefly discuss hibernation, and teach the song.

For fun and added interest, bring some of the tiny bears available at craft and other stores. Give one to each child and have the bears "crawl" under your other hand, cupped to represent the cave.

Children may be reluctant to part with the bears after the song. Let them place their bears in one area of the room to "watch" the rest of the class.

Listen, Little Brown Bear

Monica Dale

Lis-ten lit - tle brown bear, win - ter is com - ing, Snow is fal-ling and the wind is hum - ming.

Crawl in-side your cave and sleep 'til Spring,   Dream-ing of the sun-shine Spring will bring.

Moving Like Bears (Multiple)

"Do bears move fast or slow? Are they heavy or light? Can you show me?"

Let the children move freely, out of the circle formation.

Stay with the children using the drum to play twice as slow as the basic beat. Speak or sing rhythmically in response to their movement.

Encourage slow, weighted movement by giving feedback on what you see individual children doing that you want to elicit. For example, "Matthew's movement is right with the drum;" "Alice is moving like a very heavy bear;" "Taylor is taking giant steps;" etc.

Moving with the Piano

Play music for this idea. Let the children know you'll be watching them.

For example:

Continue to respond to their movement verbally. It's important to let them know you're still involved when you're at the piano.

Example — "Bears" (Multiple)

Stopping and Starting the Movement

"Sometimes the bears think they see a perfect cave for their hibernation, and they stop and freeze very still, looking at it and trying to decide."

"Then they move on again, looking for another cave."

Provide pauses in your playing that make sense with the phrasing. (Think of where a fermata would make sense and add silence there.) Cue them at first: "And they saw another cave…"

This is an exercise in "inhibition," pulling energy inward to slow down or, as in this case, ceasing movement for stillness. The idea of looking at a cave provides consciousness of visual focus.

Resuming movement is an example of "excitation," the opposite of inhibition – moving faster or, as in this case, initiating movement.

Following the Piano

"Now listen carefully to know when to stop."

Continue playing as before.

For children with previous experience in Eurhythmics, it's probably not necessary to say anything – simply continue to play with pauses and they'll follow.

Moving like Squirrels (Division)

"I saw a different kind of animal outside my window this morning. It had a bushy tail and looked like it was digging for acorns. What do you think it was?"

"Oh that's what it was, a squirrel! Are they heavy like bears or light? Do they move fast or slow? Are they big like bears with big steps? Can you show me?"

Again, play with the drum and respond to their movement to encourage small, quick steps at the division.

Sometimes children get down on all fours. If they do, don't "correct" them – they're actually correct in emulating squirrels. Instead, ask them to imagine squirrels that can scamper on their two hind legs with their front paws held in front. This image keeps their elbows at their sides, which has the effect of minimizing lower body movement as well, making the steps appropriately small and better controlled.

Moving with the Piano

Play music for this idea.

For example:

As before, provide feedback from the piano to let the children know you're still involved.

Example — "Squirrels" (Division)

Starting and Stopping the Movement

"Sometimes squirrels stop very suddenly, and hold so still that it's hard to see them."

Provide pauses between phrases.

Squirrels are actually fascinating to watch in the way they alternate from quick movement to absolute stillness. If you have a window and there are squirrels outside, let the children take a look.

Changing to Arm Movement ("Digging")

"Sometimes they stop where they are and dig in the ground for acorns."

Make sure your playing, and the children's movement, still reflect the exact division.

Play a more static idea, in a different register. For example:

Example — "Digging"

Alternating Stepping and Digging, Following the Piano

Play phrases to include stopping, starting, and "digging."

Have the children follow the music.

You might begin with verbal cues such as "They stop!" and "Then they dig!" Then make your comments *follow* the children's responses to the music instead of preceding them. For example, after they are still: "Ah, they're so still I can hardly see them." While they are already digging: "They're working hard to find those acorns."

Alternating Division and Multiple, Following the Piano

Play the bears (multiple) idea again. "Now who moves this way?... Yes, the bears are back."

Change to the squirrel (division) idea. "Ah, now I see squirrels again!"

Gradually allow the music to lead the children's activity, and as above, give feedback only after their responses.

Continue to include pauses for both, and the "digging" idea for the squirrels.

Story: "The Bears and the Squirrels"

Tell the story first, or let the children decide ahead of time whether they'll be bears or squirrels, and let them enact the story as you tell it from the piano.

This story reinforces perception and response to the multiple and division in the music.

The Bears and the Squirrels

It was winter, and the bears were getting sleepy. They lumbered around the forest, looking for a cave to hibernate in. Sometimes they thought they'd found a good one, and stopped to look. But it took a little while for them to find just the right cave.

Finally they found the perfect cave for their long winter's nap. *(Indicate one space in the room for the bears to gather.)* They crawled inside and went to sleep.

Along came some little squirrels, scampering quickly and lightly. Sometimes they stopped so still, they could hardly be seen. They continued on, until they found places to dig for acorns. *(Play for "digging" as before.)* But they didn't find any, and kept going, getting hungrier and hungrier.

Without even realizing it, they scampered closer and closer to the bear's cave until they were right in front of it. They started digging for acorns there. They were so hungry they dug with a lot of energy, and it made a loud sound…

Uh-oh! Their digging woke up the sleeping bears! The bears came lumbering out of their cave, slow and sleepy and grumpy, wondering who woke them up! They growled:

The squirrels were scared! How could they get the bears to go back to sleep? They had an idea – maybe if they sang the bears a lullaby…

(apologies to Brahms)

The bears yawned and stretched, then slowly walked back to their cave, crawled inside, and went back to sleep. And the squirrels scampered away.

Following the Music Only

After a time or two, have the children enact the story without any words, carefully following the music.

Repeat so that the children have an opportunity to take both roles.

Adding the Beat (Deer)

"One day in the forest, a beautiful family of deer came walking by. They had long necks and long legs that stepped carefully and gracefully, lifting their feet high off the ground with each step. Can you show me?"

Step with them at the beat, using the drum and your voice to elicit a smooth walk.

Lifting the knees and feet helps children to sense the space and time.

Moving with the Piano

Go to the piano as they are stepping and transfer the idea to music.

For example:

Try making the transition seamless – keep speaking rhythmically and playing the drum as you move to the piano.

Replace the drum with the piano as quickly as possible.

Example: "Deer" (Beat)

Alternating Between Beat, Division, and Multiple

Alternate between the three ideas, providing cues as needed for the children to change their movement, as before.

For example, "Whose music is this now?" If they don't need these cues, simply respond to what they're doing with encouraging feedback.

Responding to the Piano with Individual Roles

"The bears *stomp,* the squirrels *scamper,* the deer *step.* What letter do all those words begin with?"

This helps them to identify "S" for "Space" to be used in notation later.

Have the children form a horizontal line at one end of the room. They "secretly" decide for themselves whether they'll be a bear, squirrel, or deer.

When they hear their music, they are to move straight across the room to the other side.

This approach allows the movement to travel in a long linear direction across the room.

Identifying and Remembering Movement

Ask the children to point out who the bears were, who were squirrels, and who were deer.

This encourages children's attention to the movement of others, and is an exercise in memory.

Repeat so that children have an opportunity to change roles.

Responding to Visual Signals

Introduce three arm signals to indicate the three movements. For example:

Holding your arms low in front of you, with hands parallel to the floor, means "Bears," identified and chanted as "Long."

Holding your arms with elbows bent, hands at waist level, means "Deer," identified and chanted as "Beat" or "Walk."

Holding your arms high over your head means "Squirrels" identified and chanted as "Short."

Palms facing the children at mid-level means "Stop."

With the children lined up as before, bring them forward using these arm positions.

Introduce them one at a time, letting the children follow them, rather than explaining all at once. For example, "Slow" then "Stop" several times; "Beat" then "Stop" several times; alternate "Beat," "Slow" and "Stop"; then add "Fast."

It's important to use your voice in this exercise, singing or speaking rhythmically, to provide musical sound.

If they seem ready. let children try leading as well, while you provide music with the piano or drum.

Transferring Movement to Sound

Bring the children back to a circle, seated. Have them use their hands as "feet" on the floor, "stepping" at the division, beat and multiple in response to your arm signals as above.

Ask them to listen carefully to the sound they make together on the floor.

Transfer the sound to a light clap.

Here they are continuing movement, but making a natural transfer to sound.

Notation

Have a set of cards prepared (large index cards work fine), notated with the beat, division, and multiple.

Explain that these are the music notes that tell us what to do, just as we read letters and words that tell us what to say.

Hold a beat note card at mid-level and identify it as "walk, walk" or "beat, beat," pointing along the notes as you chant, and have the children say it with you.

Hold a division note card high overhead, identifying and chanting it in the same way as "short short short short."

Hold a multiple note card low, identifying and chanting it as "long."

Continue in varying order with the children clapping the durations notated. Then help them respond to the notation without holding them at the three spatial levels.

For example, one each with two half notes, four quarter notes, and eight eighth notes.

Using the same three levels of space as in the earlier exercise eases the transition to notation.

Here they are following only the notation, without the cue from the levels in space.

Pitch: Stepping the Scale

Have the children line up horizontally once more. They imagine they're stepping up a ladder that is lying on the floor, taking eight steps forward. As they do, sing the ascending scale on numbers, with or without the piano.

Then reverse – have them step backwards with a descending scale, singing from 8 to 1.

Be sure they sing with you.

Stepping in Spaces

Lay five pieces of ribbon across the floor horizontally, like a large staff.

Let the children help – align them in two facing rows of five, with others in the center (for classes of more than ten). Give each outer child an end of the ribbon to hold, and the centers to the middle children.

Then have them place the ropes down, evenly spaced with less than a foot between them, and then carefully step between them to return to one side of the room.

Next, from their horizontal line, have the children step carefully into the first space, then the second, third and fourth. Then reverse, fourth space to first space.

Alternatively, use heavy yarn or other material. Be sure to use a color that contrasts with the floor and can lie fairly flat, to be stepped on later. Tape and chalk work, but are unkind to the floor. You could also give them the ribbons while they're in random order and then move them to their rows.

Here's an opportunity to extend the task into a related exercise: before they step aside, have them lift and lower the ropes together, singing up and down the scale.

Play or sing appropriately in 3rds, ascending and descending.

Identifying Spaces

Step (or jump) into one of the spaces, and ask the children to identify whether you're in the first, second, third, or fourth space.

Then let the children lead: either individually or in small groups, they step/jump into spaces, and others to identify which space each is in.

This is why the ribbons can't be placed too far apart – the fourth space should be close enough to jump to, even if it's challenging.

"Notating" Spaces with Bodies

Call a space number for the children to step or jump into.

Then have them jump back through all skipped spaces, as others identify them ("Three, two, one, off!").

If it's crowded, have only some children move at a time. For example, "Everyone wearing red, jump to the third space."

12

Supplementary Worksheets

If time permits, give the children pencils and copies of Worksheet 1 and help them draw notes in spaces as directed; or, give them the sheets to complete at home.

Directions are written on the sheets for the parents to help the children.

Ending Song

Bring the children back to the circle where they began the lesson. Sing the ending song together.

The ending song provides a comforting ritual for transitioning to the end of the lesson.

Ending Song

Melody: "Frere Jaques"
Lyrics: Monica Dale

In our cir - cle, in our cir - cle, Low and high, low and high,

I will see you next time, I will see you next time. Wave good-bye, wave good-bye.

Suggested movements:

Ms. 1-2: Circle arms parallel to the floor.
Ms. 3-4: Reach arms down to the legs and then high.
Ms. 5-6: Lightly tap each others' feet.
Ms. 7-8: Wave with one hand and then the other.

Rhythmic movement is a very focus of energy and joy. † 13

Emile Jaques-Dalcroze

Lesson Two

Anapest

Beat and division are combined into binary anapest rhythm (short-short-long);
Alternations of beat, division, and anapest; Identification of movement and notation;
Reinforcement of space-note identification; Solfege syllables from "do" to "la."

Materials

1. Set of cards showing beat, division, and anapest, with optional illustrations of characters (more cards than the number of children in the class).

2. Supplementary Worksheets, #2 (optional)

Lesson Two: Anapest

Outline

I. Warm-up with anapest ....Preparation; introduction of rhythm

II. Song: "January"
    A. Sing, clap rhythm ....Experience and awareness of rhythmic phrase
    B. Clapping/identifying rhythmic pattern ....Isolating/developing awareness of pattern

III. Finding the pattern in other songs
    A. "Frere Jaques," "Jingle Bells" (optional) ....Linking new experience with familiar ones
    B. "Twinkle, Twinkle" / "January Weather"
        1. Clapping on the pattern ....Isolating and identifying the pattern
        2. Movements for entire song ....Distinguishing division and anapest
        3. Finding new movements ....Reinforcement, creative participation
        4. Stepping the song ....Locomotor experience of the rhythmic phrase

IV. Focusing on pattern continuously
    A. Finding new movements ....Creative participation;
        further kinesthetic experience
    B. Stepping as squirrels ....Refining movement technique

V. Building Snowmen
    A. Long phrase ....Establishing focal point in space; low level
    B. Medium-length phrase ....Return to spatial point; mid-level
    C. Short phrase ....Return to spatial point; high level
    D. Patting and smoothing the snowman ....Re-experiencing anapest

VI. Song: "The Snowman"
    A. Walking as snowmen ....Locomotor experience of beat; association
        with music
    B. Melting ....Gradual change of level through phrase
    C. Creating other movements (optional) ....Creative participation

VII. Beat, Division, and Anapest with music
    A. Prancing as horses ....Locomotor experience of division
    B. Alternating with snowmen ....Differentiates beat and division
    C. Anapest as squirrels ....Differentiates rhythm, beat and division
    D. Alternating three patterns ....Aural perception; quick reaction

VIII. Story: "The Snowmen, Horses and Squirrels"
    A. Choosing roles ....Isolating and distinguishing three patterns
    B. With the drum and words ....Reinforces rhythmic experience, quick
        reaction
    C. With the piano ....Aural perception, quick reaction

IX. Notation
    A. Identifying patterns with words ....Links notation to kinesthetic experience
    B. Choosing one card to determine story roles ....Reading notation
    C. Identifying others' movement ....Visual perception; awareness of others;
        memory

X. Worksheets (optional) ....Reinforces rhythm reading;
        space notes from Lesson One.

XI. Ending song
    A. Singing 1-6 on numbers, solfege syllables ....Develops vocabulary for pitch awareness/
        studies
    B. Singing song with numbers ....Develops melodic awareness toward notation
    C. Finding and moving on anapest ....Relates new experience with familiar song

Lesson Two: Anapest

Warm-Up

Keeping a moderate beat tempo, provide exercises using the Anapest rhythmic pattern (short-short-long).

For example:

See the introduction for explanation of rhythmic modes.

Notice that any two-movement exercises alternate, as in the example below.

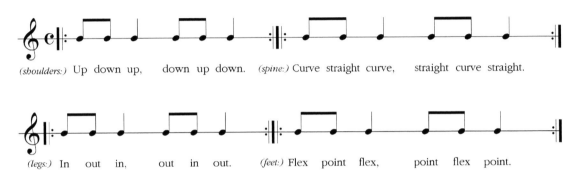

(shoulders:) Up down up,   down up down.   *(spine:)* Curve straight curve,   straight curve straight.

(legs:) In   out   in,   out   in   out.   *(feet:)* Flex   point   flex,   point   flex   point.

Song: "January"

Ask the children what month it is. Tell them when they learn this song, they will know how to spell "January."

Young children are eager to learn to spell and proud of mastering a word.

January

Monica Dale[1]

J - A - N - U - A - R - Y,   J - A - N - U - A - R - Y.

[1] Based on a rhythmic phrase found in: Grace C. Nash and Janice Rapley, *Holidays & Special Days* (Van Nuys, CA: Alfred Publishing Co., 1988) p. 82

Clapping with the Song

Sing again, clapping the rhythm of the song.

Help them find ways to express the long "U" in their clapping – a large circle, a sliding movement, etc.

Isolating Anapest

"That last part makes a pattern. Let's figure out what it is."

Clap and sing "A-R-Y..." several times, then use the words "short, short, long."

As an option, point out the pattern's faster occurrence at the beginning of the song, as well. Clap and sing "J-A-N" several times, then again using the words "short, short, long." This demonstrates that the pattern can occur at different tempi.

Finding Anapest in Other Songs

"That pattern happens in 'Twinkle Twinkle Little Star', too. Let's sing it and clap every time it happens."

Sing "Twinkle" and clap on the Anapest pattern that ends each phrase.

Alternative words are provided as another option.

Find the pattern in other songs as well, such as "Jingle Bells" and "Frere Jaques."

You might also try reversing: clap with the song *except* where the pattern occurs.

Twinkle or January Weather — Clapping Anapest

Twin-kle, twin-kle, lit-tle star, how I won-der what you are. Up a-bove the world so high,
It's the chil-ly time of year, Jan-u-a-ry wea-ther's here. Get your mit-tens and your hat,

like a dia-mond in the sky. Twin-kle, twin-kle, lit-tle star, how I won-der what you are.
make a snow-man round and fat. It's the chil-ly time of year, Jan-u-a-ry wea-ther's here.

Isolating Anapest

Try silencing the words and let the sound of the clap carry the rhythm alone. (In other words, "Don't sing when you clap.")

Then as an option, try reversing: clap the divisions without singing, then sing the pattern.

Distinguishing Division and Anapest

Provide another movement for the divisions (for example, tapping knees). Sing the song with the new movement for the divisions, and still clapping when the anapest pattern occurs.

Other examples: bouncing knees, shaking shoulders, or dropping head from side to side.

Finding New Movements for Divisions and Anapest

Have the children provide new movements for the song: one for the division, and one for the anapest pattern.

Any movements they might suggest that involve standing — such as jumping, for example — will make a nice transition to the next exercise.

Stepping the Rhythm

Sing "Twinkle" again, and have the children step the rhythm of the pattern each time it occurs.

Do this along with the children. The technique will be refined later.

Then add claps on the divisions ("Clap every note where you don't step").

If it helps, change the words to fit the actions: "clap clap clap clap, step step step."

Try reversing: Step on the first part, and clap on the pattern.

Again, sing the actions if the children have difficulty.

Performing Anapest Continuously

"Now let's keep going with the short-short-long pattern. Can you do the pattern with your feet? With your head? With your shoulders? Can you jump the pattern? Who has another way?"

Repeat each idea several times, using your voice, the drum, and/or the piano.

"Can you do two ways at once — jump and drop your head side to side at the same time?

18

Stepping the Pattern Continuously

Have the children be squirrels as in Lesson One, but this time the squirrels stop every three steps to look for acorns.

This stepping technique, halting the movement on the long duration, is the easiest for children to perform, especially at a brisk tempo. It can be conveyed as "go, go, look," or even "go, go, stop."

Other words to convey the idea are "Squirrel-ly steps" (or "Hun-gry Squirrels").

(The articulation changes in this "halting" technique, but because the beat duration remains the same length, the pattern is still anapest. Think of it as a staccato articulation.)

The children have already stepped the pattern within the song – here it is performed continuously, and given greater focus. Deriving the pattern from the "squirrel" divisions in Lesson One relates anapest directly to the division and builds upon previous experience in stepping and stopping divisions.

Two alternative approaches: use a marching technique, with the leg staying up on the third step; or, imagine snow has fallen all over the room, and here and there it has drifted into deep piles. Step, step, and then step lifting the leg high over the snow-drift. While more difficult, this keeps the leg moving continuously on the long duration.

Rolling Snowballs: Long Phrase

"Now imagine the room is filled with snow. We're going to build snowmen. First we need to make a very large snowball for the bottom part. So let's roll the snow eight times."

With the children, roll imaginary snow low along the floor with your arms, stepping forward on the beat.

This activity provides further experience of steady beat, while relating varying dimensions of time and space.

Spatial Points, Low Level

"Now decide where you're going to build your snowman. Pick up your huge, heavy snowball and take it to your very own place in the room…. And put it down."

The children are using one place as a spatial focal point.

Medium-Length Phrase, Center Level

"We need a medium-sized snowball for the middle part, so we don't have to roll the snow as many times. How many times should we roll it this time?"

Imagining the three sizes creates a visual image of the relationship between time and space.

Accept any number less than eight, and greater than one. Again, "roll" in even, long durations, pick up the snowball, and return it to the same space as before.

"Where does this one go? Show me how high it is."

Here the children are recalling their focal point in the space.

Constructing the snowman also provides imagery for movement in three spatial levels.

Short Phrase, High Level

"Now what do we need? Oh yes, the head. That one can be smaller, so we don't have to roll it many times. How many times would work?"

Repeat the process, with everyone returning to their specific space in the room.

"How high is the head placed on your snowman?"

Accept any number smaller than the previous one.

Revisiting Anapest

"The snowmen need to be packed and smoothed out to make them stronger and smoother. So let's use our pattern. Pat-pat-smooooth...Pat-pat-smooooth..."

Encourage children to apply this to all levels of the snowmen.

Creating Details

"What else does your snowman need?"

Let the children pretend to add whatever details they envision.

Song: "The Snowman"

"Now imagine you *are* the snowman! Stand right in the place where your snowman is and become the snowman yourself. You're very fat and round!"

"Here's a song about you. Let's see what happens."

Sing the song on the opposite page, and walk with the children (at a moderate beat) when the snowman walks. Let them "melt" to the floor at the end.

Use the piano arrangement on pages 78-79 in Appendix One, or make up your own accompaniment with steady beats for walking.

Sometimes children like to make up movements for the rest of the song, as well.

20

The Snowman

Monica Dale

A   snow-man stood in the yard one day with a   hat u-pon his head.   I

thought   he'd   stay   for the whole   long   day,   but he   walked a-way in-stead.   He

walked a-round the block,   he   walked down to the store,   he   walked a-round the town,   then he

walked a-round some more.   He   walked down to the park,   he   walked so far and then,   he

fin-ally turned a-round, and he walked back home a-gain.   The sun came out and the air grew warm and you

know what hap-pened then,   he   melt-ed down, to the ground, 'til the day it snowed a-gain.

Division (Horses)

"I noticed that the snowmen were so big and heavy and round, they couldn't walk very fast. But while they were out walking around, they met some horses who trotted in fast, prancing steps. Can you trot in fast, prancing steps?"

Make sure they aren't running, with large steps and a lot of forward momentum, but rather lifting their knees and feet upward.

Play the drum and move with the children. Articulate the divisions with words: "Pranc-ing hors-es."

Prancing with the Piano

Transition to the piano and provide prancing music for the horses.

An example follows.

Example — Prancing Horses

Alternate Division with Beat

"Now be the snowmen again."

Play with the beat, singing or saying the word "Snow-men" in time and remarking upon their movement.

For example:

Comment to point out the differences between the beat and division ("Yes, they're much slower than the horses.")

Example — Snowman Steps

Responding to the Music

Alternate between phrases of beat and division, and guide the children to perceive and follow the piano music.

It helps to continue chanting or singing the words associated with the patterns ("snow-men," "pranc-ing hors-es") but try to leave off the words as soon as possible to let the music lead the exercise.

Adding Anapest

"And what about the squirrels?"

Play with anapest, adding words "Squirrel-ly Steps."

An example follows.

Help them recreate their movement from earlier in the class ("go, go, look").

(Or, be people stepping over snowdrifts or marching if that was preferable earlier. Change the articulation accordingly.)

Example — Squirrelly Steps (Anapest)

Alternating Beat, Division, and Anapest

Continue to lead the children's movement between beat, division, and anapest at the piano.

Story: "The Snowmen, Horses and Squirrels"

Let the children enact all the roles of the story the first time, chanting the words with you as they move.

This story provides experience in distinguishing and performing the three rhythmic ideas: beat, division, and anapest.

Again, use people stepping over the snow drifts instead of squirrels if that idea was preferable.

The Snowmen, Horses and Squirrels

One very snowy day, I went for a walk in the woods. I'd heard there were some special walking snowmen out there and I wanted to find them. But they were nowhere to be seen.

So I tried calling to them with my drum. *[Play divisions on the drum.]* No snowmen came out, but do you know what happened? Some prancing horses came out of nowhere! I'd been calling them instead! Pranc-ing hor-ses, pranc-ing hor-ses….

And when I stopped, they stopped and stood very still.

They were beautiful horses. But where were the snowmen? So I tried again. *[Play anapest on the drum.]* No snowmen came out, but do you know what happened? Some squirrels came out of nowhere! I'd been calling them instead! They were taking quick steps and stopping, as if they were looking for acorns. Go-go-look, Squirrel-ly steps, squirrel-ly steps....

And when I stopped, they stopped and stood very still.

The squirrels were so cute! But where were the snowmen? So I tried once more. *[Play beats on the drum.]* Snow-men, snow-men... It worked! The snowmen came walking out where I could see them! Snow-men, snow-men...

And when I stopped, they stopped and stood very still.

Then I decided to call someone else. Who am I calling now? *[Play divisions or anapest and help the children identify the pattern. Continue, changing roles.]*

After a time or two, use the piano to "call" them instead of the drum. Then as soon as possible, leave out the words and let the music lead the story.

One way to enact this story is to have children on one horizontal line at the end of the room. The music calls them forward in a straight line. Another way is to have them start at the perimeter of the room, and come into the center area when they are called.

This gives a linear sense to the movement and is a little like the old children's game "Mother May I." I wouldn't give them the idea that it's a race, however, or they'll distort their movement to take large steps.

Have the children perform all three roles, or choose one each time the story is repeated.

Don't repeat the story too many times at this point. Leave them wanting more, as it will be returned to with notation, below.

Notation

Have cards prepared (such as index cards) with some with two beats, some with four divisions, and some with anapest (two divisions and one beat).

Hold the cards up one at a time for the children to identify. Point along the rhythmic pattern while chanting each one ("pranc-ing hor-ses," "snow-men," or "squirrel-ly steps").

Chant the patterns in "short" and "long," and help the children discover how the short and long notes look different.

Use either quarter note beats and eighth note divisions, or half note beats and quarter note divisions. Either way is fine, as the relationship between the durations is the important matter; however, I would stay with whatever beat unit was used in Lesson One, and skip (or alter) the Supplementary Worksheet if you use half note beats.

As an option, add an illustration to each card depicting the character corresponding to the written rhythmic pattern (squirrel, horse, or snowman).

Illustration — Rhythmic Notation Cards

Snowman   Prancing Horses   Squirrelly Steps

Identifying Roles

Have each child choose one card to determine their role, and repeat the story again.

They can choose the cards "face down" and keep them secret.

At the end, see if they can identify which children had which roles, and check their cards to see if they're correct.

This requires children to identify the rhythmic patterns and perform them correctly. The game lets you gauge their abilities.

Pitch: Solfege Syllables from Do to La

Sing the scale tones from 1 to 6, ascending and descending, on numbers. Then teach (or review) singing the pitches on solfege syllables.

You might include the "ladder climbing" or gestures from *Six Lessons for Fall.*

Supplementary Worksheets

Give the children Worksheet 2, in class or afterwards, to help reinforce the rhythmic experience and further develop the skills in writing space notes from Lesson One.

Alter the worksheet as necessary if you vary the "squirrelly steps" to another idea or use a different beat unit, so that it relates directly to the children's experience.

Ending Song

Help the children to sing the ending song on numbers. (I leave the ending with the words "wave goodbye" to avoid explaining the "5" below "1".)

Singing on numbers relates the song to the context of the scale, and prepares for melodic notation.

Help the children find the "short-short-long" (anapest) pattern in the ending song.

Select one of the movements from the lesson to perform on the pattern.

Rhythmic gymnastics starts from the principle that the body is the inseparable ally of the mind; it affirms that body and mind should harmoniously perform their divers functions, not only separately but simultaneously. † 108

Emile Jaques-Dalcroze

Lesson Three

Three Compound Rhythmic Patterns

Experiences of beat, division and the trochaic rhythmic mode in compound meter (6/8), whether introductory or as a review from "Six Lessons for Fall," Lesson Five; children draw to represent the patterns, and the drawings are transferred to iconic notation; introduction of notation on lines.

Materials

1. Plain paper (three sheets for each child plus extra)

2. Markers or crayons

3. Three music stands or other means of holding three sheets of paper or charts

4. Five lengths of ribbon as used in Lesson One

5. Optional: pennies and paper with five parallel lines drawn (or use writing sheet #3)

6. Supplementary Worksheets, #3 (optional)

Lesson Three: Three Compound Rhythmic Patterns

Outline

I. Warm-up in compound meter ....Preparation; introduction of rhythms, meter

II. Skating
    A. With drum and teacher ....Locomotor experience of the compound beat
    B. Stop/start ....Quick reactions (excitation/inhibition)
    C. With piano ....Association with music; perception of phrase

III. Tippytoes
    A. With drum and teacher ....Locomotor experience of compound division
    B. Alternating with beat ....Quick reactions; differentiating beat/division
    C. With the piano ....Association with music
    D. Alternating with beat, with the piano ....Aural perception of beat and division;
        quick reactions

IV. Galloping
    A. With the piano ....Locomotor experience of trochaic rhythm;
        association with music
    B. Alternating beat, division, and trochaic ....Aural perception; quick reactions

V. Follow the Leader ....Individual improvised phrases with patterns;
        movement perception; awareness of others

VI. Transferring to sound
    A. Beat, from floor to clap ....Kinesthetic to aural performance of beat
    B. Division, from floor to clap ....Kinesthetic to aural performance of division
    C. Trochaic, from floor to clap ....Kinesthetic to aural performance of trochaic
    D. Alternations ....Quick reactions; distinguishing pattern

VII. Link to visual representation
    A. Gestures "painting" in space ....Kinesthetic experience with imagined visual
        element
    B. Drawing on paper ....Kinesthetic experience creating visual
        element
    C. Holding up in response to music ....Reconnects visual representations to sound
    D. Sharing images, tracing with fingers ....Reconnects kinesthetic, aural and visual
        experience
    E. Distilling icons from drawings ....Links above experiences to single common
        icon
    F. Alternating in response to icons ....Icons as visual representation of
        sound/movement

VIII. Story: "The Lost Children and Sleeping Giant"
    A. With words ....Association with music in sequence of events
    B. With piano only ....Aural perception of music leads physical
        response

IX. Pitch Notation
    A. Reviewing spaces ....Reinforces earlier experiences before new
        ideas
    B. Adding lines ....Transferring known skills to new concepts
    C. Pennies game ....Notating lines and spaces by number
    D. Worksheets (optional) ....Continuation of ideas for reinforcement

X. Ending song
    A. Review singing 1-6 on numbers, syllables ....Reinforcement of earlier experience
    B. Review singing song with numbers ....Reinforcement of earlier experience
    C. Singing song on solfege syllables ....Transferring known skills to new ones

Lesson Three: Three Compound Rhythmic Patterns

Warm-Up

Provide warm-up exercises in compound meter, both in your voice and body.

Embody the physical sense of compound meter yourself, even before the lesson begins.

For example:

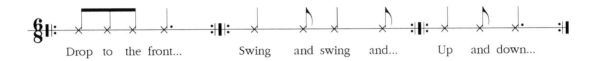

Include standing swings – arms and body swinging side to side, in and out, forward and up.

Swings naturally impart the feeling of compound meter.

Skating (The Compound Beat)

Ask the children if they've ever ice-skated, or would know how. Have them pretend the floor is all ice, and show you how they'd skate, one or a few at a time.

Imagining skating elicits the perfect physical experience of the compound meter beat.

With feedback, encourage long sliding steps with bent knees, arms swinging side to side. Have all "skate" this way along with you, and play the drum while improvising rhythmic chanting or singing as a way to continue eliciting the movement.

Often children add turns and other elaborations in their "skating," which is fun and fine. Just continue to emphasize the basic beat duration so that it doesn't get lost.

For example:

Example — Improvised Singing for Skating

Ska - ting,   ska - ting,   I   like   the way   you   bend   your knees.

Long   steps,   slid - ing,   look   at how   Jor - dan   swings   his arms.

Stopping and Starting

"Now stop and freeze into an ice statue!"

Observe and remark upon the features of the children's various body positions. Then continue skating and freezing.

Comment, for example, on their levels, shapes, and other attributes. This helps develop their awareness of themselves and each other.

Skating with the Piano

Transition to the piano and play for the compound beat.

For example:

"Let's find out what skating music sounds like." Or "I'm going to add music so I can watch you better."

Example — Skating (Beat)

Starting and Stopping with the Piano

Remind them that when they hear the music stop, they are to freeze into an ice statue.

Have them test their balance by standing on one leg, and then "on their toes" (heels off the floor).

(If they lose their balance a bit and start to take small steps to stay on the balls of their feet, pick up on that for a nice segue into the next exercise.)

What if children get "silly" and make a game of purposely losing their balance and falling to the floor? When a behavior starts that's not dangerous but yet not germane, you can either take a moment to go with it ("Can you fall sideways, forward? Slowly/quickly? What shapes do you make when you land?"), or ignore it and comment instead on what you want to encourage ("Wow, Kaley is so good at balancing she stays totally still until it's time to step again!").

"Tippytoes" (Division of the Beat)

"Now instead of balancing, can you stay up on your toes and take tiny steps?"

Play light divisions on the drum and again chant or sing rhythmically.

An example follows.

A dropping and lifting movement for the steps may be preferable at more advanced levels, but for young children this technique is a much easier expression of the divisions.

Example — Chanting with the Division

Tip - py - toe, tip - py - toe,   ti - ny steps, up on your toes...

Alternating Beat and Division

"Now change back to skating... And tippytoes again..."

Alternate using the drum, continuing to move with them and provide verbal feedback.

When working with the drum, it's important to use your voice to convey long durations, since the sound of the drum is short. In addition, try sliding your hand along the drum head instead of only striking it.

Moving Divisions with the Piano

"Let's find out how tippytoe music sounds."

Play divisions at the piano. For example:

Note that the bass and melody move within small intervals. This helps to elicit small steps.

Example — Tippytoes (Division)

Alternating Beat and Division with the Piano

"Now listen and if you hear skating music, change back to skating."

Alternate, using phrases that make musical sense.

In other words, change at cadences.

Gallop (Trochaic Pattern)

"One more pattern for today. Who knows how to gallop?" Let the children gallop as you play.

(Galloping is so natural that I use the piano right away rather than starting with the drum. The piano also gives more impetus to the movement.)

An example for improvisation follows.

Children love to gallop! While skipping is also an appropriate technique, galloping is simply easier at this level.

Another approach is simply to play for galloping and ask the children to move to the music. Most will gallop, so that all you need to do is identify it.

Example — Galloping (Trochaic Rhythm)

Alternating Beat, Division, and Trochaic Pattern

"Now listen and show me what you hear."

Return to the beat (skate). Continue alternating, with the children following the music.

Keep the basic tempo the same for all three patterns.

Follow the Leader: Your Lead

"That was like follow-the-leader. You followed the piano music, and it was the leader. Now follow me and I'll be the leader."

Have the children line up behind you, and lead them in a short phrase alternating skate, tippytoe, and gallop.

Travel all around the room in varied floor patterns, avoiding a circle (otherwise some "followers" can end up in front of the "leader").

Your being the leader is only to demonstrate the activity the first time.

Rather than playing the drum, you might hold a shaker or bells – something that essentially plays in the rhythm of the movement automatically. (Then let the child leader hold it when it's their turn.)

Follow the Leader: Their Lead

"Let's have someone else be the leader now, and we'll all follow you. Even the piano will follow you."

At the piano, play for the movement you see the children performing.

Keep the turns fairly short so more children get to lead. (You determine their length with a clear closing cadence.)

You might participate a time or two before going to the piano.

Sometimes a child will simply perform one movement endlessly, fascinated with the general idea of everyone following. That's okay, but you can also encourage or remind the child verbally ("You could change to galloping whenever you want to and we'll all follow.")

Transferring the Movements to Sound: Beat

Gather the children back to a seated circle. Have them imagine their hands are their "new feet." Skate them along the floor in a sliding motion.

"Be very quiet and listen carefully, and you'll hear a sound we're making together …. Can you make a sound like that?"

"Let's try clapping that sound."

Again, begin by chanting or singing rhythmically ("skate, skate, long slides…")

Their sounds might be "Shhh" or "whoosh," for example.

One way to clap is with a sliding motion, moving one hand across the other and then out into a circle.

Transferring the Movements to Sound: Division

"How would you make your new feet tippytoe on the floor?"

"Listen carefully so we're all together, and see if you can hear the sound it makes…. How would you clap that sound?"

A usual response is to tap with fingertips. Again, use your voice at first to encourage the right durations in relation to the beat you just did.

Any sort of light clap is fine.

Transferring the Movements to Sound: Trochaic

"Now let's gallop with our new feet…"

"And listen to the sound…"

"And clap that rhythm."

("Gallop, gallop, long-short, long-short…")

Point out how the "Long-short" makes the hands clap "Big-small" or "Up-down."

Alternating with Clapping and Voice

Call alternations between "tippytoe," "skate" and "gallop," having the children chant the words along with you.

For variety, it's fine to do this using small percussion instruments, as well.

Gestures in Space: Beat

"Imagine you have an invisible paintbrush in your hand, and a big invisible easel in front of you."

"Let your paintbrush skate in the air on your invisible easel. Not a picture, just let it skate with the music. Ready?"

Play "skating" music as before, and comment on the movement ("I see lots of long, curvy lines!").

You can have the children decide what color paint they're using to help them visualize the idea.

Sometimes I give the instructions to begin each pattern while playing the piano with just my left hand, and using my right hand to demonstrate the "painting." Then I add the right hand when it's time for the to children begin.

32

Gestures in Space: Division

"Now make your paintbrush tiptoe in the air."

Play for divisions as before.

Remark on how different it looks from skating.

("Get a new color if you want to.")

Let the children tell you what their space-paintings looks like, too. ("I made dots!" "Mine are toothpicks.")

Gestures in Space: Trochaic Rhythm

"Which one is left?... Yes, now gallop on the page in the air."

Play for galloping as before.

("Ready with a new color?")

Provide rhythmic words as you did when they were clapping ("up-down").

Transferring to Images

"Now let's make real drawings on paper."

Give each child three sheets of blank paper and and let them choose from an assortment of markers or crayons.

Repeat the process above, having them move the markers on the paper with your piano music.

(Give an introduction to each phrase, perhaps just the rhythm in your bassline, as the children "draw" with their markers in space as before; then with a "ready, go" have them directly transfer the movements to the page as you play.)

This approach lets them transfer their movement experience to a visual representation that makes sense to them.

Make observations about each drawing.

Give them a chance to change markers or crayons so that each of their three drawings will be a different color.

Sharing Images in Response to Music

Play for the skating idea, and have the children hold up their drawings so all can see them.

"Now show me your drawing for this one." Have them change which drawing they're holding up when you change which pattern you're playing.

In addition, you might have them trade pages with each other and use their fingers to trace the drawings along with the music.

At this point, the drawings are a first form of rhythmic notation. As the children look at each others' pages, they relate the images they see to the music they hear.

In a sense, this is also a quick-reaction exercise in which the children are "notating" what they hear.

Tracing their fingers along the drawing reconnects kinesthetic experience in relation to sound and visual images.

Distilling Icons from the Images: Skate (Beat)

Using three music stands or the shelf of a blackboard, prop up three new sheets of paper.

"Let's get one small idea for the skate pattern. I saw lots of long curvy lines in your drawings. So I'm going to draw just one of those long curved lines here."

Using a marker, draw one curved line similar to ones you saw in their drawings.

It might look something like the following.

This is a way to reduce the drawn icons to one pattern per page.

Example — Skate Icon

"That will stand for 'skate.'"

Slide your finger across the image chanting "skate, skate, skate" a few times with the children.

Distilling Icons from the Images: Tippytoe (Divisions)

"This page will have just one idea for 'tippytoe'. Let's use three of those dots like you drew…. "

It might look something like this:

Example — Tippytoe Icon

— — —

Again, tap your finger across the page a few times chanting "Tip-py-toe" with the children.

Distilling Icons from the Images: Gallop (Trochaic)

"We need a gallop. You drew different kinds of long-short, up-down shapes, some like zig-zags and some with points on them. So let's use something like that."

An example:

Example — Gallop Icon

34

Again, show them how the icon represents the rhythm by moving your finger across it a few times, chanting "Gallop" and "long-short."

Alternating in Response to Icons

Change quickly between the patterns, leading the children to chant and clap in response.

If you have music stands to use, try to stand behind them and point from above, from your right to your left.

Story: "The Lost Children and the Sleeping Giant"

This story is designed to integrate and reinforce the three patterns.

While the story is written about "children," they could instead be any other kinds of creatures or animals (see explanation at right).

Tell it first, or have the children move from the start while you play the drum or piano.

I often begin by saying, "Once upon a time, there were..." Then I count them aloud so they'll know I'm talking about them. "There were twelve little...." Pause if you'd like to elicit a new option for other characters besides "children" — a child will almost always finish the sentence spontaneously (twelve little gnomes, mice, etc.).

The Lost Children and the Sleeping Giant

Once upon a time, there were *(X number)* children who lived together with their mother *(or father)* in a little house right in the middle of a forest. One day, the children wanted to go out to play in the forest. Their mother said, "Alright, you can go out and play today, but be very careful, because you don't want to end up near the castle of the sleeping giant!"

So the children went out to play. They pranced, they turned, they leaped, they danced all around the great forest...

Suddenly, they realized they were lost! They'd been having so much fun, they forgot to be careful of where they were going. They were at a large pond of ice. Maybe their house was on the other side. But how could they get across the ice?

Yes, they skated across the ice, gliding, sliding, turning, going backwards, going forwards... until they finally made it to the other side.

There at the other end of the pond stood *(X number)* little horses, one for each of them. Maybe the horses knew the way home! So they each got on one of the horses, and off they went. Galloping, galloping, the horses went on their way...

Suddenly the horses stopped and let the children off. Oh no! The horses had taken them right in front of the castle of the sleeping giant! They could hear him snoring. But far off in the distance, they could see their little house. How could they get home without waking the giant?

Yes, they tip-toed very carefully... Tippytoe, tippytoe, quietly, carefully...

Suddenly they heard the giant waking up, growling! They ran the rest of the way home. Whew! They all made it back safely.

Their mother asked, "What happened? You didn't get lost, did you?" What did they say?

Play for the rhythmic patterns as before, and add other ideas — anything suitable for the first dance in the forest, bass motifs for the giant's snores and his growling when he wakes up.

Repeat the story without words, requiring the children to respond to the music only.

Finish each section with a clear cadence.

It also helps to provide little transitions, such as an upward glissando for the frozen ice, an accented diminished seventh chord when they realize they're in front of the castle, etc.

Reviewing Spaces

Set up five parallel pieces of rope or tape as in Lesson One. Review jumping to spaces by number called.

Adding Lines

Have the children step across the five lines, while saying their numbers from one to five.

Call various line numbers for the children to jump or step to.

Use the words "in the line" (rather than "on the line").

Here is the reason it's best to use something that lies flat. Thick rope, for example, is hard for little feet to step on.

This wording helps with notation later. "On the line" tends to lead children to place notes in the space above, in the way that words are written "on" lines.

Pennies Game

Give each child a penny and a page with five lines spaced 3/4" apart (or use Writing Sheet 3). Call line and space numbers for them to place their pennies in.

Be sure to check what they've done and help those who need it.

Supplementary Worksheets

Worksheet 3 provides further reinforcement of lines and spaces, with the pennies game to be played at home.

They can choose the cards "face down" and keep them secret.

This requires children to identify the rhythmic patterns and perform them correctly. The game lets you gauge their abilities.

Ending Song

Review singing scale tones from 1 to 6, and then on syllables from "do" to "la."

Review the ending song on numbers, then help the children to sing it using solfege syllables.

Solfege is a significant tool for later music studies. It's a wonderful gift to give to your students at these early ages.

Children are not taught to feel rhythm, but are merely told the signs that indicate it, the result being that the child becomes familiar with the effects of movement rather than with movement itself. Children learn to classify and name the various divisions of time; they acquire no personal experience of these divisions....The whole body should come under the educational influence of rhythm... † 109

Emile Jaques-Dalcroze

Lesson Four

Compound Rhythmic Patterns
With Notation

Links experiences from Lesson Three with notation; combines patterns into rhythmic phrases; beginning experiences in identifying, notating, and reading phrases; identification of lines and spaces

Materials

1. Cards approximately 7" x 11", with one pattern each written on them, and yarn strung through them (as many as there are children in the class).

2. Mailboxes

3. Paper hearts with patterns on them

4. Blackboard or large paper

4. Supplementary Worksheets, #4 (optional)

Lesson Four: Compound Rhythmic Patterns with Notation

Outline

I. Warm-up in compound meter ....Preparation; re-establishes compound meter

II. Song: "Valentine's Day, singing/clapping ....Vocal/melodic experience of three patterns

III. Reviewing three patterns
    A. Division (first measure) ....Reinforces physical/aural association
    B. Trochaic (third measure) ....Reinforces physical/aural association
    C. Beat (fifth and sixth measures) ....Reinforces physical/aural association
    D. Alternating with the piano ....Aural perception; quick reactions

IV. Transferring icons to notation
    A. Reviewing the three icons, chanting/singing .....Reconnects prior experience, visual
        perception
    B. Substituting music notation cards ....Transfers musical meaning to music notation
    C. Alternating between three patterns ....Reading notation, quick reactions
    D. Wearing the cards ....Physical performance in response to notation;
        aural perception; quick reactions

V. Rhythmic phrases
    A. Reading ....Performance in response to notation
    B. Notating with cards ....Aural perception, pattern identification

VI. Game: Find Some Friends
    A. Free movement ....Individual improvisation in movement
    B. Forming groups ....Social integration
    C. Reading ....Performance in response to notation

VII. Story: "Valentines in the Mail"
    A. Identifying patterns ....Recognition of notation individually
    B. Performing patterns in movement ....Performance in response to notation
    C. Identifying others' patterns ....Visual perception, awareness of others

VIII. Identifying lines and spaces by number ....Visual perception of notation

IX. Worksheets (optional) ....Reinforces skills and concepts

X. Ending song with solfege syllables ....Reinforces skills and concepts, melodic
    awareness

Lesson Three: Three Compound Rhythmic Patterns

Warm-Up

As in Lesson Three, warm up in compound meter.

Song: "Valentine's Day"

Teach the song.

Then with the children, clap the rhythm of the words while singing.

They may even recognize the rhythmic patterns right away.

Valentine's Day

Monica Dale

Va-len-tine's, Va-len-tine's, Va-len-tine's Day,   Send-ing cards out on their way.

Don't   for - get   them,   Va - len-tine's, Va - len-tine's, Va - len-tine's Day.

Review of Patterns: Division

Isolate the words "Valentine's, Valentine's."

"That's like a pattern we did last week. Who remembers what it was?"

Have the children move ("tippytoe") as you improvise at the piano or with the drum, singing or chanting "Valentine's."

Before developing familiar ideas toward new skills and concepts, it's a good idea to begin with a review of those previously-experienced ideas – moving from the known to the unknown.

A singable phrase the children can catch onto is to link the first two measures with the last two, replacing "day" with "Valentine's."

40

Review of Patterns: Trochaic

"What about this one? (Clap and say) Send-ing cards out…"

Help the children recall the "long-short" pattern as "gallop," and move with the words and the drum or piano.

You can make a repeatable motif to improvise upon by using the pitches for "sending cards out" and then continue the rhythm but with the pitches in reverse.

Review of Patterns: Beat

"And there's one more. Don't for-get them… Yes, that's just like the skating we did last week."

"Skate" with the words, "Don't for-get them."

The descending scale tones make a singable motif – try following the pitches of the song with three repetitions, ech beginning a step lower than the last; then you might start on B and ascend the same way.

Alternating with the Piano

"Let's see if you can tell which one to do, just by listening to the piano."

Alternate between rhythms, changing with the phrasing.

This is a continuation of review, but in a slightly new context.

Review of Icons: Beat

"Last week, we made some drawings for each of the patterns. Which one was this?"

Place the "skate" icon from Lesson Three on a music stand as before. Lead the children in chanting or singing "Don't for-get them" and then "Skate, skate," while moving their hands on the floor as in the previous lesson, or clapping.

I often find that children begin to clap the patterns spontaneously.

Be sure their vocal sound reflects the long duration, and doesn't stop short.

Review of Icons: Division

"And which one was this?"

Repeat the process for the divisions' icon, with "Valentine, valentine" and "Tippytoe, tippytoe."

Again, listen to the vocal sound of the chant and encourage a musical sound. Sometimes in their enthusiasm to show their skill and knowledge, children begin shouting.

Review of Icons: Trochaic

"Which one is left?"

Re-introduce the icon for the gallop rhythm, using "Send-ing cards out" and "gallop, gallop."

Here the emphasis is on the first syllable, where the pitch of the voice is higher than the second. As you inflect this way, they will follow. (Otherwise, a higher pitch on the short duration makes it become accented.)

Transferring to Music Notation: Beat

"Now here's how they look in music writing. Just like the pictures, these notes tell us what to do."

Start with "Skate" and replace the icon with a prepared card with the dotted quarter note written on it. "This is one long note that stands for skate..."

Trace your hand across the card chanting "long" and then "skate," and have the children clap and say "skate" with you.

(The cards can be cut from posterboard, approximately 7" x 11". Use a hole-punch to cut holes about an inch from the two upper corners, then take about 2 feet of yarn and thread each end through the holes, knotting them. Make enough so that there's one for each student.)

Children at this age are learning to read. Explain that it's just like reading letters and words tell us what to say – in music, the writing tells us what to sing or play, and how to do it.

Draw the dotted quarter at the left side of the card, so children can see that the duration begins there and continues through the space moving left to right.

You could also use the words in the song ("Don't for-get them").

(I don't explain the theory behind the notation at this point, but it's fine to point out a few features of the notes. While it's difficult to explain that the dot means the note is divisible by three, you might say it makes it extra-long to compare it later with the quarter note in the trochaic rhythm.)

Illustration — Wearable Cards

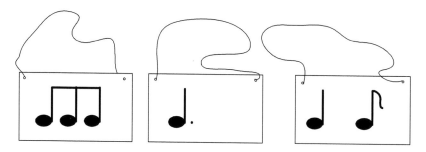

Transferring to Music Notation: Division

Replace the "tippytoe" icon with a card showing three beamed eighth-notes. "These are three short notes that stand for tippytoe."

("The beam across the top here tells us that the notes are shorter or faster than ones that don't have a beam like this. That's how these stand for short-short-short, tippytoe.")

Again, point to the notes in rhythm chanting "short, short, short" and then "tippytoe," as the children clap and chant along with you.

Return to "skate," and change back and forth a few times.

("Valentine, Valentine.")

Transferring to Notation: Trochaic

"Now here's the one for gallop."

("This is a long note, but without a dot, so it's not as long as skate; and this one has a flag on top that makes it short, just like the beams do. That's how this shows the pattern long-short, gal-lop.")

Replace the icon with a card showing the quarter note and eighth note.

Once more, point to the notes in rhythm – "long, short" and then "gallop".

("Send-ing cards out.")

Be sure to leave space between the two note values. Align them according to the divisions' card (place the quarter note where the first eighth note of the divisions began, and the eighth note in the place of the third division).

Alternating with Notation

Point along the rhythm patterns, changing between them, to lead the children in clapping and chanting.

Allow children to take turns leading this exercise.

This reinforces the link from the earlier iconic notation, and ensures transfer of their physical experience to musical meaning of the notation.

Isolating the Patterns

Turn all of the cards over, and have each child choose one. Help them to "wear" the cards by putting the yarn over their heads, so that the cards are on their fronts, with the notation visible.

Play alternating between the rhythmic ideas. The children move the pattern of their card when they hear their music played; at other times, they are still (or "frozen").

Repeat, trading cards so that children can change roles.

Do NOT let them put the cards on their backs or the yarn will be dangerously hooked around the front of their necks!

Have children move around the stationary children.

Wearing the cards allows children to see the notation moving in action, and lets you check for understanding. (In fact, children often prompt and correct each other.)

As an option, have the still children clap the other patterns along with your music.

Perceiving Patterns in Movement

If you think the children are ready, have them wear the cards backwards so that their patterns are "secret." At the end of each game, they then identify which children had each pattern.

In addition to leading children to perceive rhythmic patterns in other children's movement, this requires children to be self-reliant in identifying their cards and relating their notation to the music.

Reading Rhythmic Phrases

Have two children with different cards stand next to each other, side by side. Reading their rhythms from left to right, lead the class in clapping and chanting the short phrase their cards create.

Continue, grouping three children, and then four.

Again, give them opportunities to trade their cards for new ones.

Notating Rhythmic Phrases

Play rhythmic combinations on the piano, with clear articulation. Help the children to identify what they hear.

Then have them identify children wearing the appropriate cards to stand side by side notating the phrase from left to right. Have all perform the phrase, clapping and chanting.

Begin with just two and progress to three and then perhaps four patterns.

This is more difficult. Relating the rhythms to the words used earlier makes it easier in the beginning.

Game: "Find Some Friends"

As you improvise in compound meter, let the children dance freely around the room with their cards. On a signal, they are to form little groups of two, three, or four (depending on how many patterns were successfully read in the previous exercise.)

Then have them arrange themselves side by side. All perform the phrase each group creates.

The signal can be verbal (such as simply, "Find some friends!") or musical (such as a change of register).

For greater challenge with older children, have them wear their cards backwards so others cannot see them. They create the phrase, perform it themselves, and the class identifies their three cards.

Story: "Valentines in the Mail"

Prepare the story by giving each child a "mailbox" with a flag that can move up and down.

Have them find their own space at the perimeter of the room for their "home," leaving the central space (the "town center") clear.

Have small hearts cut from colored paper, each with one of the three rhythmic patterns written on it.

Tell the story as the children enact it.

You can make them from tissue boxes, or purchase inexpensive metal ones from Oriental Trading Company (www.oriental.com, 1-800-228-2269). An illustration follows the story.

The story is essentially a description of an exercise but the context engages children's imaginations and enthusiasm.

Illustration — Paper Heart and Mailbox

Valentines in the Mail

Once there was a town called Heartsville. On Valentine's Day, everyone in Heartsville waited by their mailboxes, with the mailbox flags up. Finally the mail carrier came and delivered some special Valentines. The flags were moved down after the mail was delivered.

The Valentine cards had special codes on them that told the people who their secret Valentines were. The codes were actually musical rhythms. Some were tippytoe rhythms, some were skating rhythms, and some were gallop rhythms.

When everyone got their mail, they opened their Valentines to see what special code they received. They put the flags on their mailboxes back up again.

Then they went out of their houses into the town center, where each person stepped the rhythm of their special Valentine code.

When they found someone else who was stepping in the same way, they became special Valentines. They joined up and went around the town together, looking for more people who were moving their way. Whenever they found someone else moving with their rhythm, they joined together until there was a whole group of them together. Then there were three groups of special Valentines in Heartsville.

Each group formed their own little circle. They showed each other their cards. Did they all match?

Then each group found a new way to do their rhythm to show everyone else what was on their Valentine's cards. Some clapped their hands, some used their arms, some used their feet, some did their rhythms with their heads.

Then they delivered their Valentine cards to someone else's empty mailbox. When they went back home, they found a new card in their mailbox. Maybe it was the same one, or maybe it was different.

Go find out!

Help the children to group together according to their rhythms.

Go to one group at a time and have them perform their rhythmic pattern. Ask the other children to identify the group's pattern, and show the cards to confirm their answer.

Guide them, if needed, in coming up with a new way to perform their rhythmic pattern.

At the end, they redistribute their cards to other children's mailboxes. Remind them to put the flags down after putting their cards inside. That way, they can see which are already full and which they can choose from to put their cards in.

For a large class, have children deliver their cards a few at a time.

Identifying Lines and Spaces

Using the blackboard or large paper with five lines, draw notes and ask the children to identify the line or space number.

As an option, try also giving them line or space numbers and help them to draw the corresponding notes.

Supplementary Worksheets

Worksheet 4 provides reinforcement of drawing notes on lines and spaces, and the rhythm patterns of this lesson.

Ending Song

Review the song with solfege syllables as in Lesson Three.

Each movement or series of bodily movements corresponds to a note-value or group of note-values, so that if the master teaches, together with the movement, the traditional music sign which expresses it graphically...at the end of two years the child will easily have learned all the usual metrical notational signs, and will be capable of experiencing the sensations of time and energy which the sight of them calls up, as well as of interpreting them either plastically by gesture or musically by the voice... †133

Emile Jaques-Dalcroze

Lesson Five

Meter of Three

Introductory experiences placing steady beat into a metric structure of three;
exercises to distinguish the crusic beat; further work on identifying line and space notes

Materials

1. Pairs of mittens cut from construction paper, with five lines and matching notes

2. Triangle instrument (optional)

3. Supplementary Worksheets, #5 (optional)

Lesson Five: Meter of Three

Outline

I. Warm-up in simple meter of three ....Preparation; introduces the meter

II. Song: "The Cats' Waltz"
    A. Singing ....Melodic/vocal experience of meter
    B. Stepping with hands on floor ....Small motor experience of beats; directions
    C. Stepping to the song ....Large motor experience of beats; directions

III. Triangles
    A. Painting the triangles in space ....Creating image of three durations, meter
    B. Clapping in corners ....Performing beats with awareness of meter
    C. Clapping with the song ....Relating song to metric awareness
    D. Silencing all but beat one ....Isolating the crusis
    E. New sounds on beats two and three ....Differentiating the crusis

IV. Experiencing the meter without the triangle
    A. Two sounds for beat 1 and beats 2 and 3 ....Differentiating the crusis
    B. Moving in the meter ....Kinesthetic experience of meter
    C. Creating new ways ....Creative participation; reinforcement
    D. Stepping the beats ....Locomotor experience of meter

V. Isolating the three beats
    A. All move only beat 1, 2, then 3 ....Isolating beats
    B. Groups perform either beat 1, 2, or 3 ....Isolating and differentiating beats
    C. Individuals choose a beat to move/sound ....Isolating and differentiating beats

VI. Triangles through space
    A. Walking phrase in three ....Phrase; direction; measured time, space,
        energy
    B. New locomotor patterns ....Transfer to/alternate among other movements
    C. Creating new ideas ....Creative participation; reinforcement

VII. Song and Story: "The Little Kittens"
    A. Mittens ....Identifying note positions
    B. Song ....Aural/vocal experience of meter
    C. Finding new matches ....Visual perception, movement improv
    D. Identifying new notes ....Identifying note positions

VIII. Scale song in three
    A. Singing the song with ascending movement........Kinesthetic experience of scale in three
    B. Creating new movements ....Creative participation; melodic awareness

IX. Supplementary Worksheets (optional) ....Reinforces identification of note positions

X. Ending song in three ....Links new ideas with familiar song

Lesson Five: Meter of Three

Warm-Up

Provide warm-up exercises, speaking and moving in a meter of three. For example:

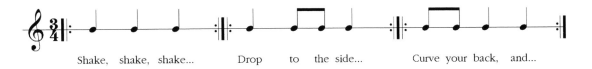

Shake, shake, shake...   Drop   to   the side...   Curve your back,   and...

Poem: "The Cat Stretch"

As an option, read the poem below and have the children move spontaneously.

Be sure to read with a sense of the meter of three.

The Cat Stretch

Monica Dale

She stretches her paws out as far as they go, then pulls them back and sits up pretty.

She rolls on the floor now, to and fro, then arches her back like a quite happy kitty.

She looks up, looks down, looks all around – she spies a tiny gray mouse!

She runs and jumps and pounces and then walks proudly back to her house.

She yawns and stretches and purrs and curls herself up in a ball very tight.

She stretches her paws and legs once more, and says "Meow," which means goodnight.

Song: "The Cats' Waltz"

Teach the children the song.

Use your hands to "step" the beats on the floor in the directions the song suggests.

Don't make the tempo too fast, or the feeling will be compound. Sense the divisions internally.

Keep the beat going, not the rhythm. Begin with hands "stepping" in three from side to side; turn around on the floor for the "turning."

The Cats' Waltz

Monica Dale

The cats went out waltz - ing one late Win - ter night. They

waltzed to the left and they waltzed to the right. They

waltzed go - ing for - ward, they waltzed go - ing back. They

waltzed turn - ing 'round then they stopped for a snack.

Stepping with the Song

Then stand and step with the children.

(Begin with steps moving side to side. Then move forward into the circle and back again, turn around, and let the children create the ending.)

To begin stepping, take a low step to the side, lift for two high steps in place, then lower to repeat on the other side. The children will not all perform this exactly yet.

"Painting" Triangles

Show the children a triangle (cut from paper, drawn on the blackboard, or drawn on paper) with one point down, as shown below.

"How many sides does it have? How many corners?"

Having the point down, and starting at the lower point, makes the crusis lift and the anacrusis fall – an important physical reality of meter and work with conducting gestures.

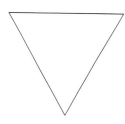

"Hold an invisible paintbrush in your hand, and we're going to paint triangles in the air. Let's start at the bottom of the triangle, right in front of you, and paint three long lines together."

Call slowly "one, two, three."

"Is your paintbrush right back where you started? Let's paint over it a few times."
Repeat painting the triangle in steady beats.

As an option, have children in pairs paint triangles as mirror images of each other.

Use your voice to convey the entire duration of each beat or "side."

Clapping in Three

"Do you have a triangle? Good! Now let's put a clap in each corner."

Again, count or chant in steady beats so that all are clapping together, vocally communicating the duration of each line and/or its division.

Do this with them, demonstrating a continued sense of movement along each line.

The lowest point of the triangle is still "1."

As an option, have them also put two claps in each corner at the division (see Lesson Six).

Relating to the Song

Point out that the cat song fits with the triangles. Sing part or all of the song while continuing to clap in the triangles.

The movement along the triangle – starting low and lifting, staying high, and then starting high and descending – is an exact transfer of the steps earlier.

Sensing the Crusis

Now clap on beat one, but make beats two and three silent claps.

Just touch fingertips together to create a "silent clap."

Adding New Sounds

Add the sound "shh" on the silent claps. Ask the children for other sounds to make instead.

This brings sound back to the metacrusis (middle beat) and anacrusis (last beat) while continuing to distinguish the crusis (first beat).

52

Sounds without the Triangle

Now use new sounds made with the body. Introduce one, and then let the children provide ideas.

For example, "Tap – slide – slide" (tapping hands on knees and sliding feet), "floor – clap – clap" (placing hands on floor at sides and clapping feet together), "brush – cheek – cheek" (brushing hand down the other arm and tapping cheeks).

If the children present an idea that doesn't make sound, either go with the silence or add a vocal or mouth sound. Always find a way to accept what they do and help modify it so that it works, rather than reject their idea.

Moving in Three

"Here's another way. Let's stand up and all pretend to push a swing into the middle of the circle."

Facing into the circle, push forward and upward on "one" and pull back on "two, three."

It isn't necessary to continue counting with numbers, but provide some sense of the beats. Sing or chant "Push – pull – back," for example.

Finding New Ways

Let the children suggest other movements.

Examples given in my classes have included throwing a ball and catching it again, swinging a baseball bat and pulling it back, and even karate movements.

Take what they give you and organize it into the meter.

Walking in Three

Reintroduce the side to side steps from the beginning of the lesson (in the song), as another example of a pattern in three ("down, up, up").

Then have the children travel as they walk.

Stay with them, using the drum and your voice.

Ideally, the walks in three begin with a step on a bent knee, rise to the second step, remain high to begin the third step and lower to start another first step. For older children, this can be introduced with low walks, high walks, and then the pattern of low-high-high. In my experience, however, this approach only complicates matters with young children.

Differentiating the Three Beats

Have the children step only on beat "one" of each measure. (Transition to the piano.)

Let them suggest a movement to do only on beat "two" of each measure (a clap, jump, kick, etc.), holding still on the other two beats.

Choose one suggestion for everyone to do.

Let them suggest a third movement to do only on beat "three" of each measure.

Groups of Three

Divide the children into three groups. Each is assigned beat one, two, or three. Have each group move only on their beat. (Adding a clap to their movement creates a sound that clarifies the activity.)

Use the drum and guide them by indicating each group in turn.

Older children can be grouped into trios ("triangles") for exercises like this one.

Rotate roles so all children experience each beat.

Of course, if the class number doesn't divide equally by 3, create a quartet or two with a pair of children doubling-up in each.

Isolating the Three Beats

Ungroup, and have each child decide whether to "be" a one, two, or three.

It's easiest to decide on one activity first – a clap or step on the particular beat, for example. Then let the children suggest other ways.

(Or, determine their roles for them: have them draw cards, or tap each child once, twice, or three times.)

Children then perform a movement or sound on their beat as you play in three.

Triangles Through Space

Set three "markers" or "bases" on the floor, equidistant from each other. (These can be shoes, folded paper cards, paper plates, etc.)

This experience conveys the notion that "one" only begins at the base, but its duration lasts through space and time all the way to "two."

Have each child walk in three from base to base in a large triangle, making clear changes of direction. (Demonstrate.)

One way is to walk 3 measures and then use the fourth measure to pivot at the corner. Set the space by taking child-sized steps as you demonstrate the first time, placing markers on the fourth measure.

Triangles through Space: New Movements

Then introduce new locomotor patterns (or have the children suggest them), one for each side of the triangle. (For example, walk from one to two; jump from two to three; hop from three to one.) Let the children give suggestions.

Play the piano to ensure clarity of the meter and phrase.

This also provides physical experience in change of direction, rhythmic experience of fitting new locomotor patterns to the meter, and involves measuring time and space to be at each base at the right time.

Mittens: Reviewing Notation of Lines and Spaces

Have sets of matched "mittens" cut from construction paper. On one side, have five lines and one whole note drawn on each. (Pairs should match.)

Show the children several pairs of mittens, and ask them to identify the line or space of the notes, as studied in previous lessons.

Relate this to jumping to lines and spaces on the floor, as performed in past lessons.

Illustration — Mittens

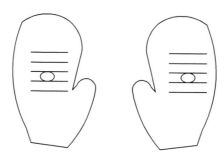

Story and Song: "The Little Kittens"

Give each child a pair of matching mittens while singing the first verse of "The Little Kittens."

Have them identify the line or space of their note.

You might begin with the song alone, and then integrate the story; or tell the story along with the song; or enact the story directly as you sing the first time, teaching the children's verses and giving directions as you go.

The song, used as the basis of the story, continues the experience of the meter.

The Little Kittens

Monica Dale

The dear lit - tle kit - tens got mu - si - cal mit - tens from

Mo - ther Cat one day, Then all of the kit - tens took

all their new mit - tens and went out - side to play.

Verse 2

They played and they pranced and they jumped and they danced and their
      Mittens they did lose,
They hurried back home so fast, knowing they must at last
      Tell their Mom the news.

Verse 3

Oh mother we're sad that we've been very bad and we
      Dropped our mittens 'round,
They're out in the yard but to match them is hard cause they're
      Mixed up on the ground.

Verse 4

You bad little kittens, you must get those mittens so
      Go back out because,
You'll find a new pair then you'll have some to wear on your
      Little kitten paws.

Verse 5

Oh mother we found all the mittens around and we
      Matched them up once more,
We looked and we looked but the ones that we took aren't the
      Ones we had before.

Story: "The Little Kittens"

As indicated on page 54, the story can be integrated after singing the song, or directly along with it.

Together, the story and song involve both the meter in 3 and identification of notes in lines and spaces.

The Little Kittens

It was a cold winter day – so cold that the kittens' mother decided they all needed mittens. So she gave them each a pair. They each had a note on them so they matched.

(First verse.)

Then the mother cat let the kittens go out to play. But while they were out, they all dropped their mittens. They were all mixed up!

(Second verse: children dance while placing their mittens face up all over the floor. They could also be placed face down, but face up makes it easier.)

The kittens went home without their mittens. They told their mother the mittens were all mixed up outside.

(Third verse.)

So their mother sent them back out to get their mittens again.

(Fourth verse; children pick up a new pair of mittens. Provide a musical interlude for extra time, if needed, to allow them to find a match.)

But instead of finding their own mittens, they each found a new matching pair. When they got home again, they told their mother cat that they didn't have the same ones she gave them. Instead they'd all been switched around!

(Fifth verse.)

Question the children about the notes on their new mittens: are they the same as what they had before? Who had mittens like these in the beginning?

If some don't match, help the children trade around to sort them out. This is itself a learning activity.

Repeat the story as many times as they like.

Scale Song in Three: "Cat in the Tree"

Begin by singing the song using your hands as paws moving up and down to reflect the scale tones.

Then have the children pretend to climb the tree to standing on the ascending scale. Let them create ways to move the rest of the song.

Be sure to show a middle position in space on the G for "down to the."

Cat in the Tree

Monica Dale

Optional: Triangle Instrument

Whether here at the end or at any other transitional point in the lesson, you might show the children a triangle instrument. Let them take turns playing it, striking each side to a steady beat.

Be sure children play it with the correct striking technique. Introducing an instrument this way, using only one and taking turns playing it with care and attention, engenders an awe and respect for the instrument. I prefer it to handing out many right away and allowing them to be treated as toys.

Supplementary Worksheets

Worksheet 5 five provides reinforcement of the lines/space matching exercise.

This one may be best for use at home as it involves cutting the mittens into small individual pieces. If you do use it in class, use dull children's scissors and provide small envelopes.

Ending Song

As an option, try singing the ending song in a meter of three, as follows. You might have the children clap in triangles while singing it.

The anapest rhythm could also be performed as three equal beats.

Ending Song: Variation in 3

In our cir - cle, in our cir - cle. Low and high, low and high.

I will see you next week, I will see you next week. Wave good-bye, wave good-bye.

The development of attention in children tends to strengthen their brain-capacity... The natural qualities which benefit by education of the attention are chiefly memory and concentration; and the best means of training the attention of children is to play intelligently with them. Games should be joy-giving; I look upon joy as the most powerful of all mental stimuli. † 100

Emile Jaques-Dalcroze

Lesson Six

Meter of Four

Placing steady beat into a metric structure of four; exercises to distinguish the crusic beat; review of division and anapest with notation; notating melodic seconds

Materials

1. Index cards, half with beats and half with anapest notated on them (one set of two for each child)

2. Five lengths of ribbon as used in previous lessons

3. Blackboard or large chart

4. Supplementary Worksheets, #6 (optional)

Lesson Six: Meter of Four

Outline

I. Warm-up in simple meter of four
  A. General movements in four ....Preparation; introduction of meter
  B. Series of movements ....Memory; coordination; corporal awareness

II. Song: "March"
  A. Rhythm ....Perception/performance of rhythm in four
  B. Song ....Combines rhythm with melody
  C. Identifying rhythmic pattern............................Isolating anapest, reinforcement
  D. Marching ....Reinforcing beat and/or rhythm

III. Squares
  A. Painting squares ....Creating image of four durations, meter
  B. Clapping in corners ....Performing beats with awareness of meter
  C. Clapping beat with song ....Relating song to metric awareness
  D. Clapping divisions ....Performing divisions with awareness of meter
  E. Alternating beat and division ....Quick reaction with metric perspective
  F. Clapping "March" rhythm ....Discovering rhythm in context of meter

IV. Notation of Rhythm
  A. Introducing two cards ....Associating performance with notation
  B. Responding to cards, ordering cards...................Rhythm reading and notation
  C. Choosing cards in response to sound ....Differentiating and notating rhythm
  D. Movement to show rhythm on card ....Reading/creatively expressing rhythm

V. Squares through space
  A. Walking phrase in four ....Direction; measured time, space, energy
  B. New directions ....Coordination; corporal awareness
  C. Creating new ideas ....Creative participation; reinforcement

VI. Differentiating the crusis
  A. In groups ....Isolating various beats
  B. Individually ....Kinesthetic experience of meter
  C. Creating new ways ....Creative participation; reinforcement

VII. Moving through phrase in four
  A. Stepping forward..Linear locomotor experience;
  combining series of measures into phrase
  B. Changing levels ....Corporal awareness; distinguishing measures
  C. With the piano ....Associating registers with levels
  D. Reversing ....Directions, cognitive analysis

VIII. Game: Getting Stuck
  A. Traveling to freeze ....Reinforcement of phrase
  B. Connecting positions with others........................Awareness of others; corporal awareness
  C. Variation ....Reinforcement; social integration

IX. Story: "The Strange Shoes" ....Improvised performance of beat in four

X. Notating melodic seconds
  A. Movement patterns on lines and spaces ....Link with metric experience
  B. Stepping seconds continuously ....Kinesthetic experience of notation
  C. Writing seconds..Transfer to notation

XI. Supplementary Worksheets (optional) ....Reinforces experience

XII. Ending song with claps on cruses............................Links new idea with familiar song

Lesson Six: Meter of Four

Warm-Up

Provide warm-up exercises in groups of four.

Try making a series of movements from head to feet. For example:

For example, tilting heads to side four times, lifting and dropping shoulders four times, etc.

This provides an exercise in memory while further establishing the meter.

Head, head, head, head,   shoul-ders shoul-ders shoul-ders shoul-ders,   clap, clap, clap, clap,

bel-ly bel-ly bel-ly bel-ly,   hips, hips, hips, hips,   knees, knees, knees, knees,   feet, feet, feet, feet,   freeze!

Or, use a standing phrase: head, shoulders, clap, belly, hips (side to side), knees (bounce), feet (jump).

Challenge the children to memorize the phrase.

Try it in reverse!

(Heads: drop side to side; shoulders: lift and drop; clap: hands; belly: shift ribs side to side or curve and straighten spine; hips: rock while sitting; knees: bounce with soles of feet together; feet: kick upwards one at a time, or clap them together; freeze: everyone holds their own ending position.)

Rhythmic Pattern: "March"

Ask the children if they know what month it is. Then teach them to spell it in rhythm, clapping:

They can start by identifying the first letter in "March."

"March" Rhythm

M - A - R - C - H

Song: "March"

Teach the song while clapping the rhythm.

One way is to clap measures from left to right, returning to the left to begin each measure.

March

Monica Dale

M - A - R - C - H.   That's the month, that's the month.   M - A - R - C - H.   Spring's a-round the cor-ner.

Reviewing Anapest

Help the children find the "short-short-long" pattern in the song ("R-C-H" and "That's the month.")

Relate the pattern to their experience in Lesson Two ("Squirrelly steps" and "little star").

Marching with the Song

"Since the song is about March, let's march with it!"

Watch whether the children step the beat or the rhythm. If you see both responses, lead them to step both ways.

For example, ask the children stepping the beat to show how they are marching, and have all step that way. Then have the children who were stepping the rhythm demonstrate, and have all follow.

"Painting" Squares

"Last week we painted triangles in the air. This week, can you show me how you'd paint a square? Let's do it together. Get your paintbrush ready…"

Guide the children with your voice and demonstration, speaking with long durations. (For example, "Up, across, down, across.) Repeat several times.

As in the previous lesson in three, children can face each other and mirror "painting" the squares. By working to stay together, they automatically take greater care to establish a definite rate of speed and clear points in space for changing direction.

Clapping in Squares

"Now let's put a clap in each corner…"

"Can you sing the song and clap in the corners at the same time?"

The square groups beats into measures of four.

This adds metric perspective to the song.

Clapping the Rhythm in the Square

"What if we clapped the letters of March in the square?"

See the illustration following.

Chant or sing and demonstrate along with them. "One corner needed two claps."

Illustration — Clapping Rhythm in Squares

A ♩   R C ♫

M ♩   H ♩

Notating the Measure

Have index cards prepared, some with two quarter notes and some with the eighth-eighth-quarter pattern. Use two cards to notate the rhythm pattern for "M-A-RCH-," pointing in rhythm as you chant.

As discussed in Lesson Two, it is also fine to use quarter notes and half notes instead.

"How do the short notes look different?"

Illustration — Cards

Reading Notation

Hold up one card at a time and have the children clap it while chanting, then let them find new ways to perform it.

They might identify them either with the "March" letters, or as "long, long" and "short-short, long."

Give each child one of each card. Have them place them in the right order for the "March" pattern.

Have point rhythmically across their notes while chanting, in order to "check and make sure they're in the right order."

This further reinforces the connection between the rhythm and its notation, and conveys left-to-right reading.

64

Identification: Aural Perception

As you play the beats or pattern continuously, have the children hold up the card that indicates what they hear.

In addition to developing aural perception, the children are using the cards to "notate" what they hear.

Identification: Performing

Mix the cards up, face down. Choose one, without showing it to the children.

"Here's what's on my card." Perform movement demonstrating the beat or rhythm continuously. Ask the children to "guess" what's on your card.

Repeat with the second pattern and new movement.

Have each child select one card, and then perform any movement to show what's on it.

You might encourage a variety of ideas by showing several other ways to perform the beat or rhythm after they've identified the card. Use arms, head, hands, jumps, steps, etc. separately or in combination.

This is an exercise not only in reading notation and performing rhythm or beat, but also in the visual perception of rhythm in movement.

Marching in Squares

Set four objects as bases (as for the triangle in Lesson Five), this time forming a square.

Demonstrate four marching steps between each base, making a clear, quick change of direction at each corner.

Have the children march individually through the square.

Begin by placing base one where you are starting the square. Take four marching steps and place the base two. Continue to place the others four steps apart.

The second child can begin when the first child has changed direction at the second "base," etc...

Changing Directions

Have the children try new marching through the square in new directions – forward, backward, and sideways. (Demonstrate.)

For example, try facing the original direction throughout the square: forward on the first side, sideways on the second, backwards on the third, sideways on the fourth.

Creating New Ways

Let the children suggest new movements to the beat.

For example, jumps from base one to two; hops from two to three; springing leaps from three to four; low sliding steps from four to one.

Differentiating the Crusis: Groups of Four

Divide the class into four groups, sitting or standing at the four bases. Each group takes a turn making a sound on their beat.

For example, the beat "one" group might clap while others make a "shh" sound.

Let them rotate to change places.

Alternatively, give each group a different set of instruments, with the strongest sounding instrument given to the group on the "one" beat. Take time for a careful introduction of each instrument first.

Differentiating the Crusis: Finding New Ways

Provide an example of a pattern that differentiates the crusis. For example, "Step, clap, clap, clap;" or swing arms forward to jump, then swing arms back, front, back; or jump landing with feet apart, then three times with feet together; etc.

Let the children find new ways and present them to the class for all to imitate.

This is an activity for which rhythm sticks can be useful. Patterns might be tapping the floor, then tapping the sticks three times together overhead; sliding one stick across the other then "walking" them three times on the floor, etc.

Phrase with Levels

Demonstrate for the class: Traveling from one side of the room to the other, take four low steps, four steps at a middle level, four high on the balls of the feet, and freeze in an improvised pose for the last measure.

(Several children can travel across at a time.)

Begin by doing it with them, then transition to the piano and play at three registers.

An example follows.

Sometimes I provide an image for this phrase such as, "The ceiling starts low and gets higher." Children have also interpreted it as "walking up three big steps."

As an option, let them decide arm positions for the three levels.

Example — Phrase with Levels

Phrase with Levels: Reverse

Try having them perform the phrase in reverse, moving backwards.

At the piano, simply reorder the measures – measure 3, 2, 1, then 4.

Game: "Getting Stuck"

Form one line so the children can perform the phrase one at a time. The first child is "stuck" in their frozen pose, until the next one catches up and somehow touches them on their pose, freeing the first child to return to the back of the line.

Continue, keeping steady time.

Demonstrate ways of connecting to another's pose from along side them and from in front of them. Otherwise, if each child stops behind the stationary person ahead of them, the traveling space will get shorter and shorter.

"Getting Stuck": Variation

Instead of the second child freeing the first one, they get "stuck" to them.

Continue until all children are in one balanced body-sculpture.

Encourage a variety of levels by having children touch the foot, knee, hand, head, etc. of another person.

Story: "The Strange Shoes"

Demonstrate the "strange shoes" the first time, changing directions every four beats.

Accompany the story with the drum or piano, playing in clear measures of four.

Not all children may be successful in changing direction every four beats. Let them experiment and experience individually, at their own levels.

The Strange Shoes

One day, all the children walked to the bus stop, as they always did. The bus was very late and they were waiting a long time. They wondered if they missed it and needed to walk all the way to school!

Suddenly, one of them found a pair of strange shoes on the ground. The shoes seemed to be calling, "Wear me! Wear me!" Maybe they would help in the long walk to school.

So one of the children put the strange shoes on. The shoes felt wonderful, like no other shoes before! He bounced in place… Then he started walking, but something very weird happened. After only four steps forward, the strange shoes made him take four steps sideways… Oh no, then they made him walk four steps backwards! Then they made him jump! Then he started hopping! All the other kids thought he'd gone crazy.

Finally he took off the shoes and gave them to someone else. "These are very strange shoes. You try them," he said.

Stepping Lines and Spaces

Set up five "lines" on the floor as in previous lessons.

Provide patterns in four for stepping through the lines and spaces. For example, Jump, hop, hop, hop on each space; or step, clap, clap, clap on each line.

Then have the children step with steady beats on each line and space, balancing on the last line for eight beats to create a symmetrical phrase.

Point out that one foot is a "line" foot, the other is the "space" foot..

Example — Ascending Phrase

Writing Line-Space Pattern (Melodic Seconds)

On the blackboard or a large chart, draw five lines and a whole note on the first line. Call children to come up one at a time and draw the next note higher, to the top line.

Then continue, with descending seconds.

Relate this to the line-space stepping that they just did.

Supplementary Worksheets

Worksheet 6 provides experience writing ascending and descending line-space notes (seconds).

Ending Song

Try adding a clap, tap on the floor, or other sound on the first beat of each measure.

Or clap beats in the square while singing.

A teacher's career is the finest of all; nevertheless, it exacts of every one of us a constant balance between our reasoning faculties and our spontaneous instincts. We have to weigh the pros and cons, to harmonize the present, past and the future, to dispense with useless thoughts and gestures, to be both serious and light-hearted, strict and lenient, imaginative and constructive, artists and artisans, doers and dreamers, teachers and pupils, ever bent on establishing equilibrium between the progress we should call forth in others and that which we should ourselves realize for the joy and security of future generations. † 246-247

Emile Jaques-Dalcroze

Appendix 1

Additional Accompaniments

The songs that follow are included in the Lessons as unaccompanied melodies to be sung without the piano. While individual lessons may or may not use the piano with these song, the arrangements in this Appendix provide the option.

For an index to songs and stories, see page 89.

Cat in the Tree

Monica Dale

The cat climbed the tall - est old tree in the town, She

climbed up so high that she could - n't climb down. Up in the

tree, she looked down at me, then jumped down to the ground.

The Cats' Waltz

Monica Dale

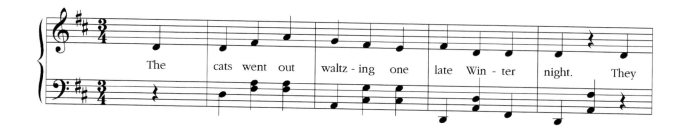

The cats went out waltz - ing one late Win - ter night. They

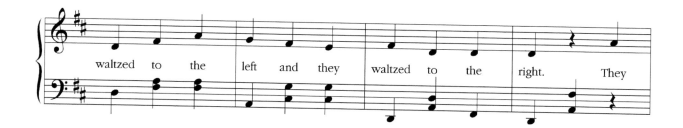

waltzed to the left and they waltzed to the right. They

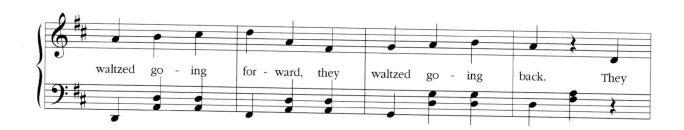

waltzed go - ing for - ward, they waltzed go - ing back. They

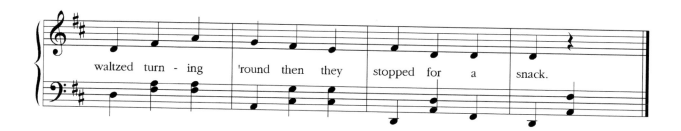

waltzed turn - ing 'round then they stopped for a snack.

Ending Song

Melody: "Frere Jaques"
Lyrics: Monica Dale

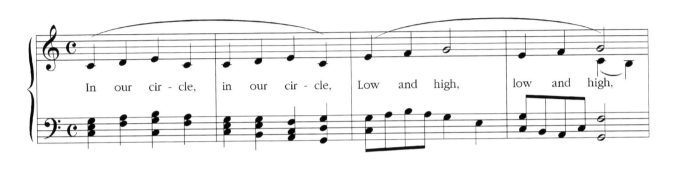

In our cir - cle, in our cir - cle, Low and high, low and high,

I will see you next time, I will see you next time. Wave good - bye, wave good - bye.

January

Monica Dale
Based on rhythmic pattern by Nash/Rapley

J - A - N - U - A - R - Y, J - A - N - U - A - R - Y.

The Little Kittens

Monica Dale

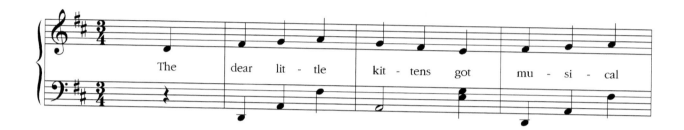

The dear lit - tle kit - tens got mu - si - cal

mit - tens from Mo - ther Cat one day,

Then all of the kit - tens took all their new

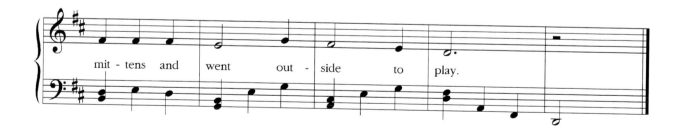

mit - tens and went out - side to play.

Verse 2

They played and they pranced and they jumped and they danced and their
    Mittens they did lose,
They hurried back home so fast, knowing they must at last
    Tell their Mom the news.

Verse 3

Oh mother we're sad that we've been very bad and we
    Dropped our mittens 'round,
They're out in the yard but to match them is hard cause they're
    Mixed up on the ground.

Verse 4

You bad little kittens, you must get those mittens so
    Go back out because,
You'll find a new pair then you'll have some to wear on your
    Little kitten paws.

Verse 5

Oh mother we found all the mittens around and we
    Matched them up once more,
We looked and we looked but the ones that we took aren't the
    Ones we had before.

Listen, Little Brown Bear

Monica Dale

Lis-ten lit - tle brown bear, win - ter is com - ing, Snow is fal-ling and the wind is hum - ming.

Crawl in-side your cave and sleep 'til Spring, Dream-ing of the sun - shine Spring will bring.

March

Monica Dale

M - A - R - C - H. That's the month, that's the month.

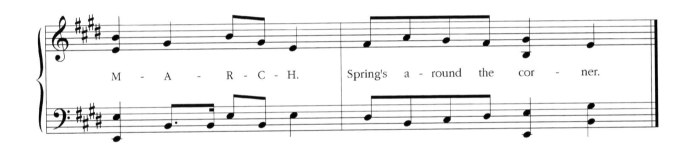

M - A - R - C - H. Spring's a - round the cor - ner.

The Snowman

Monica Dale

A snow-man stood in the yard one day with a hat u-pon his head. I

thought he'd stay for the whole long day, but he walked a-way in-stead. He walked a-round the block, he

walked down to the store, he walked a-round the town, then he walked a-round some more. He

walked down to the park, he walked so far and then, he fin-ally turned a-round, and he

walked back home a - gain. The sun came out and the air grew warm and you

know what hap - pened then, he melt - ed down, to the ground, 'til the day it snowed a - gain.

Valentine's Day

Monica Dale

Va-len-tine's, Va-len-tine's, Va-len-tine's Day, Send-ing cards out on their way.

Don't for - get them, Va-len-tine's, Va-len-tine's, Va-len-tine's Day.

Appendix 2

Supplementary Worksheets

The worksheets that follow are optional, intended to reinforce concepts and introduce rudiments of music reading and writing. Because children of the pre-school ages may not be ready to read and write, the worksheets are more appropriate for kindergarten and above.

Worksheets may be included in class, or given to children to take home and complete with an adult. As described in the Overview, the worksheets provide a springboard for children to share their experiences with their parents. The instructions on the pages are more for the adults than the children, who may or may not be able to read them.

Page xii of the introduction explains the approach to pitch notation incorporated into both the lessons and the worksheets.

1. Space Notes

How many lines are there?   How many spaces?
The footprints show how you jumped in the spaces. The oval shapes make music notes.
Trace the oval shapes around the footprints. Can you tell what number space each is in?

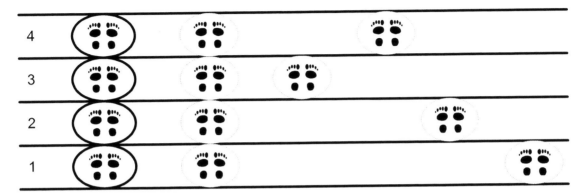

Draw your own oval shapes around these footprints.
Can you tell what number space each one is in?

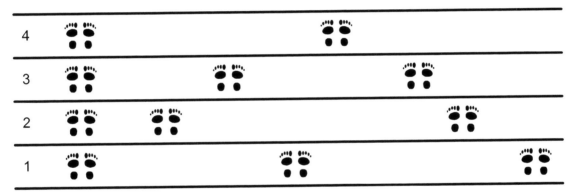

Cut out the oval notes underneath, then paste them into the spaces that match their numbers.

2. Snowmen in Spaces
Rhythmic Patterns

Here's a snowman with 3 parts, all the same size.

Trace this snowman along the dotted lines.

Can you draw another snowman?

Trace this bigger snowman. How many parts does it have?

Draw two more big snowmen.

Do you remember what these patterns are? Can you clap them with the words?
If you want to, cut them out and choose one at a time. Then show someone else how to do its movement.

"Snowman"   "Prancing Horses"   "Squirrelly Steps"

3. Snowmen in Lines
Pennies in Lines and Spaces

Here's a snowman with 3 parts, all the same size.

Trace this snowman along the dotted lines.

Can you draw another snowman in the lines?

Trace this bigger snowman. How many parts does it have?

Here's the biggest snowman of all. Trace it. How many parts does it have?

Can you draw another big snowman in the lines?

Penny Game: See if you can put a penny in the line or space number someone else tells you. Then let the other person put a penny down, and see if you can tell what number line or space it's in. (To make it harder, cover up the words and numbers on the left with a piece of paper.)

Line 5

Space 4

Line 4

Space 3

Line 3

Space 2

Line 1

Space 1

Line 2

4. Lines and Spaces
Rhythmic Patterns

Color each note, using different colors.

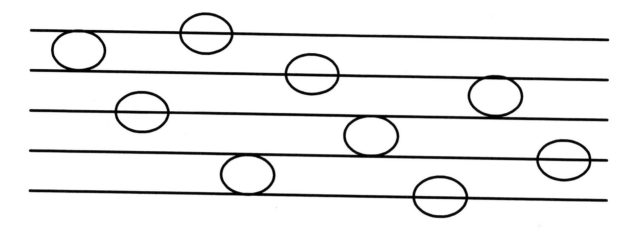

What color is the note in Line 1?   Line 2?   Line 3?   Line 4?   Line 5?

Space 1?   Space 2?   Space 3?   Space 4?

Can you clap and say these rhythms? Show someone else how you move them. If you want to, cut them out and choose one, then show how it goes.

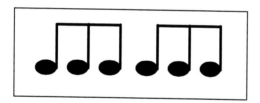

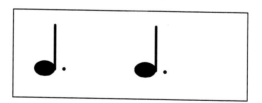

87

5. Matching Mittens
Line and Space Notes

Cut out the mitten pairs on the dotted lines.
Mix them up, then match them into pairs again.

6. Line and Space Patterns

Circle the faces to make line and space notes.
Some have dotted lines to trace to get you started.

Circle these faces the same way.
Can you see a pattern they make?

Try drawing some more notes in the line-space pattern.

Index to Songs and Stories

Songs

Stories

About the Author

Monica Dale is a leading proponent of Dalcroze Eurhythmics, as well as a dancer and pianist. She received her M.M. in Piano Performance from Ithaca College where she also earned the Dalcroze License and Certificate, and B.A. from Connecticut College. Her dance background includes training at the Martha Graham School of Contemporary Dance, the Joffrey School of Ballet, Jacob's Pillow, and the American Dance Festival. Monica lives in Maryland with her husband Michael and daughter Hilary.

More books by Monica Dale

Eurhythmics for Young Children:
    Six Lessons for Fall

Eurhythmics for Young Children:
    Six Lessons for Spring

Songs Without Yawns:
    Music for Teaching Children through Dalcroze Eurhythmics (or any method!)

Advice from the Attic:
    Perilous Pearls of Wisdom on Beauty, Charm and Etiquette

www.musikinesis.com